The Ultimate Disney Trivia Book 3

Other Books by Kevin Neary and Dave Smith

The Ultimate Disney Trivia Book
The Ultimate Disney Trivia Book 2

Other Books by Dave Smith

Disney A to Z: The Official Encyclopedia

The Ultimate Disney Trivia Book 3

Kevin Neary
and Dave Smith

New York

Library of Congress Cataloging-in-Publication Data

Neary, Kevin F.
    The ultimate Disney trivia book 3 / Kevin Neary and
Dave Smith.—
      1st ed.
        p. cm.
      ISBN 0-7868-8253-0
      1. Walt Disney Company—Miscellanea. I. Smith,
Dave, 1940–
    II. Walt Disney Company. III. Title.
    NC1766.U52D55424 1997
    741.5′0974′93—dc21   97-2506
                                      CIP

Book Design by Richard Oriolo

FIRST EDITION

10 9 8 7 6 5 4 3 2

Contents

Introduction

by Dave Smith, Archives Director,
The Walt Disney Company

It is hard to believe that it has been four years since the publication of the first *Ultimate Disney Trivia Book*. Because of its popularity, Kevin Neary and I followed up with a second book two years later. Now, with continuing support and encouragement by Disney fans around the world, we have been convinced to compile a third volume.

This third book has given us an exciting opportunity to explore areas of The Walt Disney Company that did not even exist when we prepared the first two books. As The Walt Disney Company continues to grow, expand, and open new frontiers, the possibilities for trivia questions do the same. For example, two new areas into which the company has expanded in the past few years have been in live theater and sports. As a result, we have added two new categories to this book with questions relating to Walt Disney Theatrical Productions and Disney Sports Enterprises. In addition, familiar divisions of the company such as animation, live action films, television, and the theme parks have not stood still but have experienced their own spurts of growth. New movies continue to be made, new shows appear on television, and new attractions are added at the parks. All of this adds possibilities for new trivia questions.

Since our last trivia book, Kevin Neary has moved from The Disney Store to a position with Disney Vacation Development at Walt Disney World. In 1996 Hyperion published my *Disney A to Z: The Official Encyclopedia,* a compendium of Disney facts for readers who want more detail about the individual topics that are covered in the questions and answers in this trivia book.

On October 16, 1998, The Walt Disney Company celebrates its seventy-fifth anniversary. It was on that October date in 1923 that

Walt Disney signed his first contract, and began his company. When one reaches a significant anniversary, there is always a desire to look to the past. As we reminisce about the company's lengthy history, it is appropriate that we have a new Disney trivia book to help commemorate that auspicious anniversary.

Kevin Neary came up with most of the trivia questions included in this book. We then carefully worked on them to ensure that they were straightforward and accurate. Several Disney experts were called upon to offer their insight, and the result is here before you.

In the tradition of our two previous books, this book again includes a total of 999 questions. Just like the Haunted Mansion, which claims to have 999 happy haunts and always room for one more, there is always room for one more trivia question.

Acknowledgments

We would like to take this opportunity to express our thanks to the following colleagues, friends, and family members without whose advice, cooperation, and encouragement this trivia book would not have been possible: Steven Clark, Rebecca Cline, Tyson Ervin, Collette Espino, Shelly Graham, Wendy Lefkon, Adina Lerner, Susan Neary, Monique Peterson, Andrea Recendez, Russell Schroeder, Paula Sigman, Ed Squair, and Robert Tieman.

Animated Cartoons and Featurettes

....

Questions

1. What fairy tale was the first to be adapted into a cartoon by Walt Disney?

2. Beginning in 1923, Walt Disney produced a series called the Alice Comedies. How many Alice Comedies were produced over the years?

3. What adjective is used to describe one of Walt Disney's earliest characters, a rabbit?

4. For one year Walt Disney was responsible for the Oswald series. During that time, how many Oswald cartoons did he produce?

5. Which Disney-developed animated character was the first to appear on a merchandise item?

6. What is the name of the boat landing where Mickey loads a collection of barnyard animals in the animated classic cartoon *Steamboat Willie* (1928)?

7. What two major tunes can be heard during the cartoon *Steamboat Willie* (1928)?

8. Which 1928 animated short features Mickey playing the hero, El Gaucho, who saves the beautiful Minnie, a dancer at the Cantino Argentino, from the clutches of the villainous Pete?

9. Grieg's composition *March of the Dwarfs* helped inspire the development of which Silly Symphony?

10. Besides Mickey Mouse cartoons, which other series was advertised on the Walt Disney Studios sign that towered above the Hyperion building?

11. Beginning in 1929 and continuing until 1939, Walt Disney produced a collection of cartoons called Silly Symphonies. During that ten-year span, how many Silly Symphony cartoons did he release?

12. During which decade did Mickey star in the most cartoons?

13. In *The Fire Fighters* (1930), whom does fire chief Mickey save from the top floor of a burning city skyscraper?

14. How did Pluto get his name?

15. What does Mickey discover on his doorstep one day in the 1931 animated short *Mickey's Orphans?*

16. What author wrote the classic tale *The Ugly Duckling?*

17. Mickey Mouse was credited with saving what toy manufacturer from bankruptcy?

18. How many teeth does Goofy have?

19. The music of Schubert, Rossini, and Mendelssohn are all carefully blended into which 1932 Silly Symphony?

20. What is the title of the last Silly Symphony to appear in black and white?

21. Which 1932 animated short features Mickey selling his dog Pluto to a spoiled rich kid so that he can earn enough money to give a poor family some Christmas joy?

22. Who provided the original voice for the villainous Big Bad Wolf?

23. What song includes the words "He don't take no time to play, all he does is work all day?"

24. After the success of *Three Little Pigs* (1933), three sequels were made starring the famous trio. Can you name these animated shorts?

25. Which 1933 animated short stars Mickey Mouse in the role of a jockey?

26. Which 1933 animated short featuring Mickey saving Minnie from a large gorilla was inspired by another film from that year, *King Kong?*

27. Which 1933 animated short is based on the classic story of "Jack and the Beanstalk"?

Animated Cartoons and Featurettes

28. How many cels (celluloids) does it take to make a single cartoon?

29. In the classic 1934 animated short *Grasshopper and the Ants,* what type of musical instrument does the grasshopper play?

30. What crop does Donald Duck refuse to help harvest in the 1934 animated short *The Wise Little Hen?*

31. Unlike many of his colleagues, Donald has appeared in mostly color cartoons, with the exception of three animated shorts. Can you name the only three black and white cartoons to include Donald Duck?

32. In the 1930s, the cels used in the production of Disney cartoons were made of what type of material?

33. Which 1930 short features Mickey saving Minnie from drowning?

34. What character refers to himself as "The Blue Streak"?

35. According to Goofy, what is the station's slogan in the classic short *Mickey's Service Station* (1935)?

36. To whom was the *New York Times* magazine referring in 1935 as "the best known and most popular international figure of his day"?

37. What is the title of the only Disney cartoon short to end in a question mark?

38. What is the title of the first animated short that features Mickey, Minnie, Donald, Pluto, and Goofy together in one cartoon?

39. What is noticeable about the animals ridden by the various members of the Hollywood team in the 1936 short *Mickey's Polo Team?*

40. In the animated short *Mickey's Circus* (1936), ringmaster Mickey introduces one of the circus's stars, Captain Donald Duck. What circus act does Donald present?

41. The title of which 1936 Silly Symphony coined a word that would be used nineteen years later to describe the stars of the *Mickey Mouse Club?*

42. What poem does Donald Duck attempt to recite in the 1937 animated short *Mickey's Amateurs?*

43. What type of instrument does Professor Goofy play in *Mickey's Amateurs* (1937)?

44. Which 1937 cartoon is based on a young little brave's desire and determination to become a great warrior?

45. In the classic animated short *Hawaiian Holiday* (1937), what character attempts to demonstrate his surfing expertise?

46. What type of instrument does Mickey play for Minnie during the animated short *Hawaiian Holiday* (1937)?

47. In the classic 1937 animated short *Clock Cleaners,* what kind of creature has made a home in the clock tower, much to the surprise of Mickey?

48. How do Mickey, Donald, and Goofy eventually get rid of four pesky ghosts in the old McShiver Mansion in the 1937 classic short *Lonesome Ghosts?*

49. Why does Mickey have only four fingers, or rather, three fingers and a thumb?

50. How does Donald attempt to control his trademark temper in the 1938 animated short *Self Control?*

51. Which 1938 cartoon features Donald Duck playing three different roles: himself, his guardian angel, and his evil side, the guardian devil?

52. Which 1938 animated short was inspired by a Eugene Field poem?

53. Which 1938 short features Donald and Goofy working together as partners in a business enterprise known as Donald & Goofy Trapping Company?

54. Which 1938 animated short features Donald on a camping excursion with his three nephews?

55. What is notable about the picadors, banderilleros, and alguaciles, the individuals who accompany the matador, in the animated classic *Ferdinand the Bull* (1938)?

56. What type of tree does Ferdinand the Bull prefer to sit under in the animated short in which he stars?

57. What voice did animator Milt Kahl provide for the Academy Award-winning animated short *Ferdinand the Bull* (1938)?

58. Which 1938 Silly Symphony features popular movie stars from that era, such as Katharine Hepburn, Laurel and Hardy, and W. C. Fields appearing as caricatures of fairy tale characters Little Bo Peep, Simple Simon, and Humpty Dumpty?

59. Who provided the original voice for Donald Duck's three nephews?

60. What was the only year Walt Disney released four different animated shorts that were all nominated for an Academy Award for Best Cartoon?

61. What is Donald Duck—much to his surprise—called on to deliver on Friday the 13th in the 1939 short *Donald's Lucky Day?*

62. After Mickey and Pluto are booted out of the dog show in the 1939 short *Society Dog Show,* what does Mickey place on Pluto's paws in an effort to impress the judges?

63. What is the name of Donald's inflatable horse, which he attempts to ride in the 1939 short *Beach Picnic?*

64. What is so appropriate about the clock carried by Donald's voracious cousin in the animated short *Donald's Cousin Gus* (1939)?

65. What type of creature pursues Donald and his three nephews in the 1939 animated short *Sea Scouts?*

66. Which 1939 animated short features Donald in the role of a police officer who is faced with the impossible job of presenting the evil Pete an eviction notice?

67. Beginning with the cartoon *Mr. Duck Steps Out* (1940), what affectionate nickname does Donald call Daisy?

68. What does Pluto decide to place in his own suitcase when he and Mickey take a train ride in *Mr. Mouse Takes a Trip* (1940)?

69. Who plays the railroad station baggage handler who experiences all kinds of trouble when trying to get a magician's trunk ready for the 5:15 train in *Baggage Buster* (1941)?

70. According to the song, during what "very merry" month do Mickey and Minnie take a stroll in the park, in the 1941 short *The Nifty Nineties?*

71. How does Minnie gain the attention of Mickey in *The Nifty Nineties* (1941)?

72. Taking into consideration all the bad luck experienced by Donald in the 1941 short *Truant Officer Donald,* why is the number of his badge so appropriate?

73. Which two characters join Goofy during his dancing routine in the 1941 classic animated short *Orphan's Benefit?*

74. Goofy's famous and predictable yell when danger or pitfalls come his way, "Ya-ha-ha-hoooooiieee!" is first used in which animated short?

75. Which Disney animated character appeared on the most World War II insignias?

76. What principal instrument does Donald Duck play in the classic 1942 short *Symphony Hour?*

77. With what kind of animal does Pluto match wits in order to become the new Yoo-Hoo Division Mascot for the United States Army's Camp Drafty, in the 1942 short *The Army Mascot?*

78. In *The Olympic Champ* of 1942, what happens to the Olympic torch carried into the stadium by Goofy?

79. What piece of furniture does Goofy use to help himself swim in the 1942 short *How to Swim?*

80. Which 1942 Pluto animated short features the playful pup battling a lion, a gorilla, a mother and baby kangaroo, and an alligator in an effort to retrieve a rather large bone?

81. What phrase appears on Donald Duck's badge in the 1942 animated short *Bellboy Donald?*

82. What is the title of the first animated short to feature Minnie Mouse in a solo performance without the assistance of Mickey?

83. What popular comical musician did his own version of the song "Der Fuehrer's Face" from the 1943 animated short?

84. What is the basic difference between Chip an' Dale's teeth?

85. In Italian this character is known as Pippo, in French as Dingo, and in Norwegian as Langbein. By what name does the English-speaking world affectionately know him?

86. Which 1945 animated short features characters from a book that come to life and challenge Donald's imagination?

87. What branch of the military enlists Pluto to help keep a sharp lookout for intruders in the 1945 animated short *Dog Watch?*

88. Another wartime cartoon features Pluto in *Canine Patrol* (1945). This time around, Pluto's job is to keep a vigilant watch on the beach. To which branch of the armed services is the cartoon dedicated?

89. Who is Goofy's opponent in the animated short *A Knight for a Day* (1946)?

90. What is unusual about Chip an' Dale's noses in the 1946 animated short *Squatter's Rights?*

91. What are the names of the two basketball teams that compete against each other in the 1946 animated short *Double Dribble?*

92. Who saves the day for Mickey after he forgets his and Minnie's tickets to attend the costume party dance in the animated short *Mickey's Delayed Date* (1947)?

93. In the animation process, what is the artist called who creates the basic design for a scene that is given to the background artist for painting?

94. What is Goofy's main responsibility in the 1948 short *The Big Wash?*

95. What does the two hundred refer to in the 1948 Donald Duck animated short *Tea for Two Hundred?*

96. What sport is featured in the 1949 short *Slide, Donald, Slide?*

97. In the Academy Award–nominated short *Toy Tinkers* (1949), which two characters decide to play with Donald's Christmas presents?

98. What famous playwright used the line, "thank heaven for Donald Duck"?

99. Which animated short features Chip an' Dale causing Donald grief as he attempts to ride his bicycle to Daisy's house?

100. What is the name of the dog Pluto attempts to emulate in order to impress Dinah, in the 1950 cartoon *Wonder Dog?*

101. What is the name of the enormous moose that Morris and Balsam challenge for the leadership of the moose herd in the 1950 short *Morris, the Midget Moose?*

102. Which two characters make life absolutely miserable for Donald while on vacation in the great outdoors during the 1950 animated short *Trailer Horn?*

103. Which 1950 Goofy cartoon has actually been used by police departments around the country in driver's training courses?

104. Which couple is known as Paperino and Paperina in Italian?

105. Which animated short was the first released Chip an' Dale Cartoon?

106. Which 1951 animated short features Donald's three darling nephews as teenagers?

107. Which country used to produce a product called Mickey Mouse Marmalade?

108. What kind of animal is Lambert forced to confront after this creature poses a threat to his "mother" in the animated short, *Lambert the Sheepish Lion* (1952)?

109. According to the stork's note, where should Lambert have been delivered, as opposed to where he was actually delivered, in *Lambert the Sheepish Lion* (1952)?

110. How do the townspeople show their gratitude to Goofy after he captures the villainous Pete in the animated short *Two-Gun Goofy* (1952)?

Animated Cartoons and Featurettes

111. After experiencing all types of highway problems, where does Goofy finally get the opportunity to enjoy the peace and quiet of his vacation in the 1952 animated short *Two Weeks' Vacation?*

112. According to Amos the mouse from the 1953 featurette *Ben and Me,* how many brothers and sisters does he have?

113. Which Disney character can be found on his own brand of orange juice?

114. Whom do Chip an' Dale help to capture in the Old West–themed animated short *The Lone Chipmunks* (1954)?

115. After Paul Bunyan is washed up in a cradle on the shore of a small New England town, who adopts the infant?

116. What is the salesman Joe Muffaw attempting to sell in the featurette *Paul Bunyan?*

117. According to the story, where is Paul Bunyan headed at the conclusion of the 1958 featurette?

118. What is the name of the Academy Award–nominated featurette starring Donald Duck exploring the wonderful world of mathematics with the assistance of the "Spirit of Adventure?"

119. Who portrays Mr. X, the winner of the water ski championship, in the 1961 animated short *Aquamania?*

120. What kind of animal is the Small One in the 1978 featurette by that same name?

121. In 1980, The Walt Disney Company, in an effort to promote sports as a way of achieving health and fitness, provided what cartoon character to deliver this message?

122. According to Tigger's song, what are his "tops" and "bottoms" made out of?

123. In the featurette *Winnie the Pooh and a Day for Eeyore* (1983), what is the name of the game that Winnie the Pooh invents?

124. In *Winnie the Pooh and a Day for Eeyore* (1983), what do Pooh and Piglet present to Eeyore for his birthday?

125. How many birthday candles are on top of Eeyore's cake in *Winnie the Pooh and a Day for Eeyore* (1983)?

126. Which Disney family member was the first to introduce Walt to the Pooh stories?

127. What is written on the badge worn by Jiminy Cricket in the featurette *Mickey's Christmas Carol* (1983)?

128. What is the name of the 1984 Summer Olympic mascot developed for the Los Angeles Games by a Disney artist?

129. What does Baby Herman swallow, resulting in Roger rushing him to the hospital's emergency ward during the 1989 Roger Rabbit short *Tummy Trouble?*

130. In which state do Roger and Baby Herman take the ride of their lives in the 1990 Roger Rabbit short *Roller Coaster Rabbit?*

131. Who plays the park ranger for Yellowstain National Park in the 1993 Roger Rabbit short *Trail Mix-Up?*

132. Which Tex Avery classic MGM animated cartoon character has made cameo appearances in each of the three Roger Rabbit shorts, *Tummy Trouble* (1989), *Roller Coaster Rabbit* (1990), and *Trail Mix-Up* (1993)?

133. The Walt Disney Company has teamed up with which famous filmmaker in order to bring audiences the animated character Roger Rabbit?

134. In *The Return of Jafar,* the first made-for-video sequel to *Aladdin,* who supplies the voice of the Genie?

135. How is the power of Jafar, in his form as a genie, destroyed in *The Return of Jafar,* and which character was responsible for saving the day?

136. Which actor presently provides the doglike sound effects for the character Pluto?

137. While on a camping trip with his son, what legendary creature do Goofy and his son Max encounter in *A Goofy Movie* (1995)?

138. With whom is Goofy's son Max smitten in the film *A Goofy Movie* (1995)?

139. What is the name of the first Disney animated short to be produced at a new production studio in France?

140. What is the name of the evil scientist Mickey confronts during the animated short *Runaway Brain* (1995)?

141. What is the fitting home address of the evil scientist in *Runaway Brain* (1995)?

142. In *Aladdin and the King of Thieves* (1996), the second made-for-video sequel to *Aladdin* (1992), what are the Forty Thieves searching for?

143. Which family member does Aladdin realize is still alive in *Aladdin and the King of Thieves* (1996)?

144. What very special ceremony takes place in *Aladdin and the King of Thieves* (1996)?

145. What is the name of the video sequel to the 1991 full-length animated feature *Beauty and the Beast*?

Animated Cartoons
and Featurettes

Answers

1. In 1922 Walt Disney released *Little Red Riding Hood*. The cartoon was produced in Kansas City and was part of a series Walt called Laugh-O-grams.

2. From 1923 until 1927, Walt Disney produced a total of fifty-seven Alice Comedies, one in Kansas City and fifty-six in California.

3. Oswald the "Lucky" Rabbit.

4. Walt Disney produced a total of twenty-six Oswald the Lucky Rabbit cartoons beginning in 1927.

5. Oswald the Lucky Rabbit appeared on a few buttons and school items. Mickey Mouse is credited with being the first animated character to be extensively merchandised.

6. Podunk Landing.

7. "Steamboat Bill" and "Turkey in the Straw." The animated short *Steamboat Willie* was actually inspired by a silent film, *Steamboat Bill, Jr.,* starring Buster Keaton.

8. *The Gallopin' Gaucho.*

9. *The Skeleton Dance* (1929).

10. Silly Symphonies (sound cartoons).

11. Walt Disney released a total of seventy-five Silly Symphony cartoons.

12. The 1930s showcased the largest number of cartoons featuring Mickey Mouse—a total of eighty-seven. Remarkably, there have been only 120 Mickey Mouse cartoons over the years. Of that number, about 60 percent were produced in black and white.

13. Minnie.

14. In 1930, scientist Clyde Tombaugh at the Lowell Observatory identified the existence of a new planet. In keeping with the tradition established with the other planets, it was named after a god from classical mythology, Pluto. With all the publicity about the new planet, it was inevitable that Walt Disney and his staff consider that name when their dog character made his debut the same year.

15. A basket of kittens.

16. The classic tale was written by Hans Christian Andersen. Walt Disney actually released two versions of the story in animated form, one in 1931 and another in 1939, the latter in color.

17. In 1934, the Lionel Corporation produced a Mickey and Minnie windup handcar, which sold so well that the company was saved from bankruptcy. The toy sold for $1.00.
18. Two.
19. *Flowers and Trees.*
20. *Just Dogs* was released on July 30, 1932, which coincidentally was the very same day the first color Silly Symphony, *Flowers and Trees,* was released.
21. The animated short is *Mickey's Good Deed.* By the end of the cartoon, Pluto is once again united with Mickey after the spoiled rich kid makes life miserable for the playful pup.
22. Billy Bletcher is the voice of the original Big Bad Wolf. For many years, Bletcher also provided the voice of another villainous character, Pete.
23. "Who's Afraid of the Big Bad Wolf?"
24. *The Big Bad Wolf* (1934), *Three Little Wolves* (1936), and *The Practical Pig* (1939).
25. Mickey plays a jockey for the big race in *The Steeplechase* (1933).
26. In *The Pet Store* (1933) Mickey saves the day. In one scene we see the gorilla perched on top of a pile of crates shaped like New York's Empire State Building. Mickey also saved Minnie from a gorilla in *The Gorilla Mystery* (1930).
27. Like Jack, Mickey faces a giant in *Giantland* (1933).
28. For every second of a cartoon, twenty-four frames of animation are needed, meaning twenty-four hand-painted celluloids. However, some cels are held for two frames. So, an ordinary eight-minute cartoon could have anywhere from 5,760 to 11,520 cels.
29. A fiddle.
30. He feigns a bellyache when it comes to harvesting corn, but is not so hesitant when it comes to eating it.
31. *Orphan's Benefit* (1934), *The Dognapper* (1934), and *Mickey's Service Station* (1935) were the only cartoons that Donald appeared in that were not in color.
32. Nitrate cellulose, a very unstable material, posing a potential fire risk.
33. The animated short story is *Wild Waves* (1930). At first the day started out pleasant as the two enjoyed the beach. Then the water swept Minnie away and it was up to Mickey to save her.
34. Max Hare from the classic animated short *The Tortoise and the Hare* (1935). Max Hare is no stranger to bragging; the term "blue streak" refers to the color of the dust left behind after the Hare takes off running.

35. "You Break 'em, We Fix 'em!"
36. Mickey Mouse.
37. *Who Killed Cock Robin?* (1935).
38. *On Ice* (1935).
39. The horses for the Hollywood team are caricatures of their riders; even the ostrich Harpo Marx rides resembles him.
40. Donald is responsible for a group of performing sea lions. However, the smallest sea lion is reluctant to obey Donald's authority, causing him endless grief.
41. *Three Blind Mouseketeers.*
42. Donald attempts to recite "Twinkle, Twinkle, Little Star," but he has difficulty remembering the words.
43. Professor Goofy attempts to master the "One-Man-Band," performing the song "In the Good Ol' Summertime."
44. *Little Hiawatha.* After the success of the cartoon, Walt Disney and his staff actually explored the possibility of expanding the role of Hiawatha and starring him in his own full-length animated feature.
45. Goofy, but the waves don't want to cooperate.
46. Mickey plays the ukulele while Minnie does a hula dance in her grass skirt wearing a flower lei.
47. A stork who is reluctant to leave.
48. Mickey, Donald, and Goofy represent the Ajax Ghost Exterminators. As the cartoon ends, the three accidentally collide into a combination of molasses and flour, creating their own ghostly image and giving the ghosts a taste of their own medicine by scaring them out of the mansion.
49. According to the animators the four fingers were for convenience. Apparently, no part of the human anatomy is harder for an animator to draw than a hand. It is extremely difficult not to make the hand appear disproportionately large.
50. Donald listens to a radio show that focuses on helping individuals calm their temper. However, Donald's temper gets the best of him, resulting in a smashed radio by the end of the cartoon.
51. The short is *Donald's Better Self.* After considerable battling with each side, good and evil, the guardian angel seems to have the last say as it is off to school for Donald.
52. *Wynken, Blynken and Nod.*
53. The title of the cartoon is *Polar Trappers,* featuring the two as business partners. Their slogan is WE BRING 'EM BACK ALIVE.
54. *Good Scouts.* Donald soon realizes that the great outdoors isn't

necessarily "great," after he tangles with an angry bear and the predictable Old Faithful.

55. Some are caricatures of the artists responsible for the cartoon.
56. His favorite cork tree.
57. He did one line as Ferdinand.
58. *Mother Goose Goes Hollywood.*
59. Clarence "Ducky" Nash provided the original voice for the three nephews, Huey, Dewey, and Louie. Nash is also famed for providing the voice of Donald Duck for more than fifty years.
60. In 1938 Walt Disney, remarkably, had four animated shorts all competing for Best Cartoon: *Good Scouts, Mother Goose Goes Hollywood, Brave Little Tailor,* and *Ferdinand the Bull.* "And the winner is . . . *Ferdinand the Bull.*"
61. A time bomb.
62. Mickey placed a pair of roller skates on Pluto to help demonstrate that the pup is not like any ordinary dog.
63. Seabiscuit.
64. Instead of numbers, the clock's dial indicates mealtimes: "dinner," "tea," "supper," and "lunch."
65. Donald plays admiral while his three nephews handle the difficult task of rowing the boat to avoid a vicious shark.
66. *Officer Duck.* Ironically, in the 1936 animated short *Moving Day,* it had been Pete who presented Donald and his pals with an eviction notice.
67. Toots.
68. Pluto packs his suitcase full of bones.
69. Goofy.
70. "In the very merry month of May."
71. Minnie bats her eyelashes and then drops her handkerchief in an effort to attract the attention and affection of Mickey.
72. Donald wears badge number 13.
73. Horace Horsecollar and Clarabelle Cow.
74. In the 1941 short *The Art of Skiing,* the Goofy yell is introduced, originated by Pinto Colvig, the original voice of Goofy.
75. Donald Duck.
76. Donald is the drummer, but the talented duck is also seen playing a variety of other instruments.
77. A goat named Gunther.
78. It goes out!
79. A stool.
80. *Pluto at the Zoo.*

81. "The Guest Is Always Right." Certainly even Donald has a right to question that expression after the pompous Senator Pete and his obnoxious son stay at Donald's hotel.

82. In 1942 Minnie, as a way of supporting the World War II effort, starred in the educational film *Out of the Flying Pan, Into the Firing Line.* The first regular cartoon she soloed in was *First Aiders* (1944).

83. Spike Jones.

84. Dale has two teeth that are separated and Chip's are together.

85. Goofy.

86. *Duck Pimples.*

87. The Navy enlists Pluto to keep a sharp lookout. His mission is to let no one on board, but unfortunately a little mouse (not Mickey) has other ideas.

88. The cartoon is "Dedicated to the Dogs of the U.S. Coast Guard," and it features Pluto guarding a United States Coast Guard Patrol Station.

89. Goofy, playing the role of Cedric, is an aspiring squire for Sir Loinsteak. Goofy is forced to battle Sir Cumference (also known as "Old Iron Pants") after he accidentally knocks out Sir Loinsteak.

90. They both had black noses, not the traditional black and red noses.

91. P.U. plays U.U. in a basketball showdown. Ironically, each of the players are Goofy lookalikes and they are named after Disney artists. P.U. wins!

92. Mickey's pal Pluto.

93. Layout artist.

94. To give the reluctant elephant Dolores a bath. At the conclusion of the cartoon, Dolores decides to give Goofy a wash of his own.

95. An army of ants.

96. Baseball.

97. Chip and Dale.

98. Noël Coward, in his play *Brief Encounter.*

99. *Crazy Over Daisy* (1950).

100. Prince.

101. Thunderclap.

102. Who else but Chip and Dale.

103. *Motor Mania.*

104. Donald and Daisy.

105. *Chicken in the Rough* (1951).

106. The three are featured as teenagers in the animated short *Lucky Number.*

107. England.

108. Lambert saves the life of his "mother" by confronting a hungry wolf.

109. According to the stork's note, Lambert should have gone to a mother lion in South Africa but he was mistakenly delivered to a mother sheep.

110. They make him sheriff.

111. Goofy experiences the peace, quiet, and solitude of his vacation while in jail.

112. Amos is one of twenty-six mice that live in a Pennsylvania church.

113. Donald Duck. Over the years, Donald has been featured on a variety of products ranging from drinking straws and bread, to canned vegetables.

114. Black Pete.

115. The whole town adopts the giant baby, and they give him the name Paul Bunyan.

116. Joe Muffaw is attempting to revolutionize the logging industry by introducing steam-powered saws. In a sense, he is trying to eliminate the usefulness of Paul Bunyan. Joe Muffaw organizes a competition, "Man vs. Machine—A Timber-Cutting Contest."

117. Paul Bunyan realizes he can do no more after successfully forging new frontiers across the United States. Paul Bunyan is last seen heading north, to Alaska, where he could do the most good and where he would not feel as crowded because of his big size.

118. *Donald in Mathmagic Land.* (1959).

119. The ever graceful and talented Goofy.

120. A small donkey.

121. Goofy filled the new role, helping to promote and sponsor sports of all types. Appropriately, Goofy became known as "Sport Goofy."

122. According to the song, Tigger's "tops" are made out of rubber and his "bottoms" are made out of springs.

123. One day while on the old wooden bridge, Pooh invents a game he refers to as "Pooh-Sticks."

124. Pooh gives Eeyore an old honey pot he refers to as a "useful pot" and Piglet presents a burst red balloon. Eeyore appreciates both gifts and even goes on to say that red is his favorite color.

125. Three.

126. Walt Disney's daughter Diane was the first to introduce the Pooh stories to her father.

127. It reads "Ghost of Christmas Past Official," a phrase similar to the words on Jiminy's badge as official conscience in the full-length animated feature *Pinocchio* (1940).

128. Sam the Eagle, designed by Disney artist Bob Moore.
129. A rattle.
130. Florida.
131. The beautiful Jessica Rabbit.
132. Droopy Dog. The character can also be found in the feature *Who Framed Roger Rabbit* (1988). In the feature, the voice of Droopy Dog is supplied by the movie's Director of Animation, Richard Williams.
133. Steven Spielberg.
134. Voice actor Dan Castellaneta provides the voice of the Genie. Castellaneta is perhaps best known for supplying the voice of Homer Simpson in the Fox television program *The Simpsons*. In the film's second video sequel, *Aladdin and the King of Thieves* (1996), the role of the Genie is reprised by the character's original voice, Robin Williams.
135. Iago, the parrot, saves the day by kicking Jafar's genie lamp into a pool of molten lava, thereby destroying the power of the lamp and Jafar.
136. Bill Farmer; who also provides the voice of another famous dog—Goofy!
137. The legendary Bigfoot.
138. The lovely Roxanne.
139. *Runaway Brain* (1995).
140. Actor Kelsey Grammer supplies the voice for the evil scientist, Dr. Frankenollie. The name "Frankenollie" is actually a tribute to a pair of veteran animators, Frank Thomas and Ollie Johnston, who were responsible for countless Disney projects over the years, including *Snow White and the Seven Dwarfs* (1937).
141. 1313 Lobotomy.
142. The Forty Thieves are searching for the scepter that will lead them to the fabled Hand of Midas, which turns all it touches to gold.
143. Aladdin discovers his father, Cassim, is still alive.
144. The marriage of Princess Jasmine and Aladdin.
145. *Beauty and the Beast: The Enchanted Christmas* (1997).

Comic
Characters

Comic
Characters

Questions

1. Who wrote the first Mickey Mouse comic strip, which appeared in newspapers on January 13, 1930?

2. In which year did the first Disney color comic strips appear?

3. Which company was the first to produce comic books depicting Disney animated characters in the United States?

4. Which publication was considered the forerunner of the Disney comic books?

5. Which character appeared on the front cover of the first *Walt Disney's Comics and Stories*?

6. Which famous artist has been credited with developing Donald's three nephews in comic books?

7. What is considered the hometown of Huey, Dewey, Louie, and Scrooge McDuck?

8. What is the name of the pseudo-scout organization, first introduced in comic stories, to which Huey, Dewey, and Louie belong?

9. According to the artist who drew many of the Donald Duck comic stories, how old were Donald's nephews when originally introduced?

10. What are the names of Minnie Mouse's two nieces?

11. Which comic book character is known for his invention of a baggage buggy that runs on a quart of firecrackers?

12. Which comic book character did Carl Barks refer to as a "loafer, bum, chiseler, and connoisseur of the fast buck"?

13. According to Carl Barks and his comic book stories, who is considered the second-richest duck in the world after Scrooge McDuck?

14. What are the names of Chip and Dale's two nephews?

15. Which character was featured in comic book stories with the car license plate number "313"?

Comic
Characters

1. Walt Disney wrote the first Mickey Mouse comic story that appeared in newspapers. In the story, Mickey dreams of meeting aviator Charles Lindbergh. The comic strips were distributed by King Features Syndicate.

2. Beginning in January of 1932, Mickey Mouse and the Silly Symphony comic strips were featured in color in Sunday newspapers.

3. Although many companies have produced comic books featuring Disney characters over the years, Dell Comics was the first.

4. The publication, which ran from 1935 until 1940, was known as *Mickey Mouse Magazine*.

5. Donald Duck appeared on the first issue, which was released in October 1940; it sold for ten cents.

6. Legendary artist and illustrator Carl Barks was responsible for the development of Huey, Dewey, and Louie in comic books.

7. Duckburg, U.S.A., in the state of Calisota.

8. Huey, Dewey, and Louie belong to the Junior Woodchucks.

9. According to Carl Barks, the three were depicted as mischievous five-year-olds.

10. Minnie Mouse's two nieces are named Melinda and Melodie, but they have appeared only in comic books.

11. Gyro Gearloose is responsible for the baggage buggy as well as other unique inventions.

12. Donald Duck's cousin Gladstone Gander.

13. Flintheart Glomgold, who resides in South Africa, is considered the second-richest duck in the world.

14. Chip and Dale's two nephews are named Zip and Zap, but they have appeared only in comic books.

15. The number "313" appeared on Donald Duck's car license plate in many comic book stories. Another common license plate number for Donald was "1313".

Animated Features

Snow White and the Seven Dwarfs

December 21, 1937

Questions

1. What important character from the feature *Snow White and the Seven Dwarfs* appears in only two scenes; once at the beginning and once at the end of the film?

2. After running away from the Huntsman, Snow White faces many obstacles that are not what they appear. What does Snow White believe the driftwood becomes?

3. Who helps Snow White find shelter after her encounter with the Huntsman?

4. According to the song, what else do the Dwarfs dig for besides diamonds?

5. Who is entrusted with locking the door to the diamond mine vault at the end of each workday?

6. Where is the key to the diamond mine kept?

7. Which one of the Dwarfs has the biggest belly, which one has the longest beard, and which one has the biggest nose?

8. What unpleasant task are the Dwarfs attempting to do during the song "Bluddle-Uddle-Um-Dum?"

9. Which one of the Dwarfs accidentally swallows a bar of soap?

10. Which Dwarf ties his beard into a knot while he is talking with Snow White?

11. The first night Snow White sleeps in the Dwarf's cottage, where do Grumpy, Doc, and Happy sleep?

12. What object does Dopey use as a pillow?

13. Which Dwarf continuously comes back for kisses when Snow White sends the seven off to work for the day?

14. The woodland animals begin to question the sincerity of the poor old peddler woman who visits Snow White in the Dwarfs' cottage after noticing which two creatures in a tree?

15. At the conclusion of *Snow White and the Seven Dwarfs,* Snow White kisses the Dwarfs before departing with the Prince. However, she does miss one of the Dwarfs. Which Dwarf does she miss?

Snow White
and the Seven Dwarfs

Answers

1. Although the Prince only appears in those two scenes, he is still considered a vital character. Actor Harry Stockwell, father of actor Dean Stockwell, provided the voice of the Prince.
2. Snow White thinks the driftwood becomes a group of alligators.
3. The woodland animals help Snow White find safe refuge by leading her to the cottage of the Seven Dwarfs.
4. They also dig for rubies but, in the words of the Dwarfs, "We don't know what we're diggin' for, we just dig, dig, dig-a-dig, dig."
5. Dopey is responsible for locking the door to the diamond mine vault.
6. Dopey hangs the key on a peg right outside the door.
7. Happy has the biggest belly, Sleepy the longest beard, and Grumpy the biggest nose.
8. They are attempting to wash up before dinner.
9. Dopey swallows the bar of soap and then hiccups bubbles.
10. Bashful.
11. Grumpy spends the night in a kettle, Doc sleeps in the sink, and Happy sleeps in the cupboard.
12. At first, Dopey has in his possession the only pillow in the cottage, but then the other Dwarfs tear it apart. Dopey is left with one feather, which he uses as his pillow.
13. Dopey keeps coming back for kisses.
14. The woodland animals spot two vultures in a nearby tree and thus question the real identity of the poor old peddler woman.
15. Snow White doesn't kiss Sleepy.

Pinocchio

February 7, 1940

 Questions

1. As the film opens, the character Jiminy is introduced as the narrator. Besides *Pinocchio,* what two other book titles can be seen in that opening sequence?

2. What song does Geppetto first sing about his new creation, Pinocchio?

3. What time does Geppetto go to bed?

4. What actress provided the voice of the Blue Fairy?

5. What object does Jiminy use as a makeshift parachute?

6. What lesson does Jiminy attempt to teach Pinocchio?

7. What color is the top hat worn by Jiminy Cricket?

8. What famous non-Disney actor provided the sound effects behind the character Gideon in *Pinocchio?*

9. According to Pinocchio, "I'd rather be smart" than be what?

10. As a result of his mischievous behavior while on Pleasure Island, what does Pinocchio grow as a sign that he was bad?

11. What does Jiminy use as ballast while he and Pinocchio are in search of Geppetto?

12. What type of creature does Jiminy ride while underwater as he and Pinocchio search for Geppetto?

13. After Pinocchio is transformed into a real boy, what is noticeable about his hands?

14. What animator is credited with developing the character Jiminy Cricket?

15. What major character in the Disney movie of *Pinocchio* did not have a name and was featured in only a few chapters in the original story?

Pinocchio

Answers

1. Besides the book *Pinocchio* the other two titles are *Alice in Wonderland* and *Peter Pan*. *Alice in Wonderland* and *Peter Pan* were both produced as animated features by Walt Disney and his staff more than ten years after the release of *Pinocchio*.

2. Geppetto sings the song "Little Wooden Head" to celebrate his new creation, Pinocchio the wooden puppet.

3. Geppetto, Cleo, and Figaro go to bed at 9:00 P.M.

4. Acress Evelyn Venable provided the voice of the Blue Fairy. Venable is best remembered as the live-action model of the woman holding the torch for Columbia Pictures.

5. Jiminy uses his umbrella as a parachute.

6. Jiminy attempts to teach Pinocchio to avoid temptation. According to Jiminy, temptation is "the wrong things that seem right at the time."

7. Blue with gold trim.

8. Voice actor Mel Blanc provided the sound effects for the character Gideon. Originally, a voice was recorded for Gideon, but it was decided during the course of production that the character would not speak. For years, Blanc provided many of the voices associated with the Warner Brothers Studio's characters and their Looney Tunes cartoons.

9. According to Pinocchio, "I'd rather be smart than be an actor!"

10. Pinocchio grows a tail and ears of a donkey.

11. Jiminy uses a stone.

12. Jiminy rides a sea horse.

13. After Pinocchio is transformed by the Blue Fairy, an extra finger is added to each hand to represent the fact that he is a real boy.

14. Legendary animator Ward Kimball is credited with developing Jiminy Cricket.

15. In the original story of *Pinocchio* the character Jiminy Cricket was unnamed, appeared in only a few chapters, and was squashed by Pinocchio.

Fantasia

November 13, 1940

Questions

1. Who was the only *Fantasia* composer to be alive at the time of its original release in 1940?

2. Which musical segment from the feature *Fantasia* was completed first?

3. Which individual has been credited with suggesting the title of the film *Fantasia?*

4. Which character was first suggested to play the role of the Sorcerer's Apprentice?

5. Legendary actor Bela Lugosi, known throughout his career for his role as Dracula, was the live-action model for which animated character?

Fantasia

Answers

1. Igor Stravinsky, composer of *The Rite of Spring*.

2. Dukas's *The Sorcerer's Apprentice* was the first musical sequence to be completed. Originally, *The Sorcerer's Apprentice* was planned to be released as a separate featurette. After the film was completed, however, Walt Disney realized he had spent too much money, with no chance of return if he released it just as a featurette. Walt and his colleagues then decided to produce an entire full-length animated feature.

3. After conductor Leopold Stokowski was selected to provide the musical accompaniment for the feature, he suggested the name *Fantasia* to describe the style of music.

4. Dopey, from the 1937 feature *Snow White and the Seven Dwarfs,* was originally suggested for the role of the Sorcerer's Apprentice. It was Walt Disney, however, who was determined to include Mickey as an everyman character.

5. Appropriately, Bela Lugosi served as the live-action model for the villain Chernabog in *Fantasia.*

Cinderella

February 15, 1950

Questions

1. According to Cinderella, what is the one thing even her evil stepmother can't order her to stop doing?

2. Cinderella's stepmother says that Cinderella can go to the royal ball under what two conditions?

3. What item does the Fairy Godmother almost forget to create for Cinderella in order for her to attend the royal ball?

4. The song "Bibbidi-Bobbidi-Boo" is also known by what other title?

5. According to the palace bell tower what time did the royal ball start?

6. Where does Cinderella lose her glass slipper, the one eventually recovered by the Prince?

7. What initial appears on the side of Cinderella's carriage?

8. Which character does Lucifer trap under a teacup outside Cinderella's locked tower room?

9. In the final sequence, after the marriage of the Prince and Cinderella, which character leads the royal coach?

10. The Disney version of *Cinderella* is based on a French fairy tale by what author?

Cinderella

Answers

1. According to Cinderella, "Well, there's one thing they can't order me to stop . . . dreaming."
2. According to her stepmother, Cinderella may go the royal ball provided she gets all her work done and finds something suitable to wear. Cinderella accomplishes both tasks.
3. Cinderella politely reminds the Fairy Godmother that she needs a new dress for the royal ball.
4. "The Magic Song."
5. The palace bell tower indicates the commencement of the royal ball at 8:00 P.M.
6. Cinderella loses her glass slipper on the stairs of the royal palace after she hears the bells in the tower begin to strike twelve.
7. The letter *C* appears on the side of Cinderella's carriage.
8. Lucifer traps Gus under a teacup.
9. Major the horse.
10. Author Charles Perrault and his fairy tale provided the inspiration for Disney's version of *Cinderella*. Another Perrault story was the source for Disney's *Sleeping Beauty* (1959).

Alice in Wonderland

July 28, 1951

Questions

1. According to the song "All in the Golden Afternoon," in which month is there "a wealth of happiness and romance"?

2. How tall is the caterpillar Alice meets along her journey?

3. Which character from *Alice in Wonderland* sings the song "Twas Brillig?"

4. To whom does the Cheshire Cat instruct Alice to speak first during her search for the White Rabbit?

5. Which part of the Cheshire Cat disappears last when Alice first encounters him?

6. What do the March Hare and the Mad Hatter keep offering to Alice during their celebration, but in fact never actually give to her?

7. Which character utters the words, "Twinkle, twinkle . . . little bat . . . how I wonder what you're at . . . up above the world you fly . . . Like a tea tray in the sky!"?

8. According to the Mad Hatter, how many days slow is White Rabbit's watch running?

9. What two kinds of animals serve as the croquet mallet and ball during the match between Alice and the Queen of Hearts?

10. Which three characters appear as witnesses when Alice is placed on trial for tormenting and teasing the Queen of Hearts?

Alice in Wonderland

Answers

1. According to the song, "You can learn a lot of things from the flowers, for especially in the month of June, there's a wealth of happiness and romance."

2. In the caterpillar's own words, he is "exactly three inches high." The blue caterpillar goes on to say that "it is a very good height indeed."

3. The Cheshire Cat is singing the song when Alice first encounters the troublemaking feline.

4. The Cheshire Cat instructs Alice to speak first with the Mad Hatter and then to the March Hare.

5. The Cheshire Cat's smile is the last thing to disappear.

6. The March Hare and the Mad Hatter keep pouring a cup of tea for Alice, which they never actually give her.

7. The Dormouse.

8. According to the Mad Hatter, White Rabbit's watch is running exactly two days slow.

9. The croquet mallet is a flamingo and the ball is a hedgehog.

10. In order the three are: the March Hare, the Dormouse, and the Mad Hatter.

Peter Pan

February 5, 1953

Questions

1. Who believes that Peter Pan is the "Spirit of Youth"?

2. After Peter Pan saves the life of his daughter, Tiger Lily, what name does the Indian Chief bestow on Peter Pan?

3. What is Peter Pan referring to when he says, "Once you're grown up, you can never come back"?

4. After refusing to join Captain Hook's band of pirates, who is forced to walk the plank first?

5. What eventually becomes of Captain Hook as the film concludes?

Peter Pan

Answers

1. Mrs. Darling believes Peter Pan is the "Spirit of Youth," whereas Mr. Darling has other ideas.
2. After Peter saves the life of his daughter, the Indian Chief bestows the name Little Flying Eagle on him.
3. Peter Pan is referring to Never Land.
4. The Darling children and the six Lost Boys are all taken prisoner by Captain Hook and his band of pirates; Wendy is forced to walk the plank first.
5. The last we see of Captain Hook, he is swimming frantically into the horizon, chased by the crocodile.

Lady and the Tramp

June 22, 1955

Questions

1. What happens to Lady's planned sleeping arrangements the first night she is brought into the house?

2. What are Trusty and Jock describing when they say that Lady is "wearin' the greatest honor man can bestow" and "the badge of faith and respectability"?

3. What is Jock's pure pedigree name?

4. Whom do the Siamese cats successfully blame for messing up the house?

5. What does Tramp teach Lady to chase, resulting in the two almost getting some unexpected buckshot?

Lady and the Tramp

Answers

1. An area was set aside for Lady by her owners, where she was supposed to sleep. However, she did not want to be far from her owners, Jim Dear and Darling. They mentioned that she could sleep with them that first night, but as we soon realize, one night turns into every night.
2. Trusty and Jock are describing Lady's new license and collar.
3. Jock's pure pedigree name is Heather Lad O'Glencairn.
4. The Siamese cats blame Lady for making the mess.
5. Tramp teaches Lady to chase chickens.

The Many Adventures of Winnie the Pooh

March 11, 1977

Questions

1. In the song "Winnie the Pooh," which three of Christopher Robin's friends are mentioned first?

2. According to the Pooh storybook, which two characters reside in Gloomy Place and Sandy Pit?

3. If Winnie the Pooh is apparently "stuffed with fluff," what is Eeyore stuffed with?

4. Which actor provided the original voice of Roo?

5. In which Pooh cartoon did Tigger make his debut?

6. What greeting does Pooh extend to his friends during the blustery day?

7. How many pots of honey does Winnie the Pooh attempt to rescue during the big rainstorm?

8. Which character places a message in a bottle during the big rainstorm?

9. Whose house served as the only protection during the big rainstorm in the Hundred Acre Wood?

10. Which character is thrown a "hero party" after saving Piglet?

11. When did the character Piglet make his first appearance in a Pooh cartoon?

12. According to Tigger, for whom is he saving his best bounce?

13. How is the word *honey* spelled throughout the film?

14. Which character gets lost in the woods, prompting Tigger to find him?

15. After Tigger gets stuck high in a tree, who eventually gets him down?

The Many Adventures of Winnie the Pooh

Answers

1. Eeyore, Kanga, and Little Roo are mentioned first.
2. The storybook shows Eeyore residing in his Gloomy Place and Roo playing in Sandy Pit.
3. Eeyore is stuffed with sawdust.
4. Actor Clint Howard supplied the original voice of the character Roo. Clint is the younger brother of actor-director Ron Howard.
5. Tigger made his debut in the second featurette, *Winnie the Pooh and the Blustery Day. The Many Adventures of Winnie the Pooh* is a combination of the first three Pooh featurettes assembled to make one full-length animated feature. The original plan had been to produce the story of Pooh as a full-length animated feature, but Walt Disney decided to make individual featurettes instead in order to slowly build up an American audience for Winnie the Pooh.
6. Instead of a traditional greeting, Winnie the Pooh replies, "Happy Winds-day" during the blustery day.
7. Winnie the Pooh attempts to rescue ten pots of honey.
8. Piglet places a message in a bottle that reads "Help! P-P-Piglet (Me)." Roo recovers the bottle.
9. Christopher Robin's house was the only house that did not suffer the effects of the big rainstorm.
10. Winnie the Pooh is thrown a "hero party" after saving Piglet. However, Piglet is also honored after donating his house to Owl.
11. Piglet is featured in the storybook at the beginning of the first Pooh cartoon. *Winnie the Pooh and the Honey Tree.* However, he was not introduced officially until the second cartoon, *Winnie the Pooh and the Blustery Day.*
12. Tigger is saving his best bounce for Rabbit, to whom he refers as "old long ears." However, Rabbit does not hold the same affection for being bounced.
13. "Hunny."
14. Rabbit gets lost in the woods and Tigger finds him. What Tigger did not realize is that Rabbit was trying to get Tigger lost but the plan backfired. Winnie the Pooh and Piglet were also with Rabbit but they found their own way home by letting Pooh's hungry belly lead them back to his honey.
15. The narrator helps Tigger out of the tree by tipping the book and causing him to slide down the page.

The Little Mermaid

November 17, 1989

Questions

1. In one of the film's first scenes, Ariel and Flounder are swimming frantically away from what type of creature?

2. What does King Triton want Ariel to refrain from doing, prompting him to make the statement, "As long as you live under my ocean, obey my rules"?

3. Whom does Prince Eric affectionately call an "old beanpole"?

4. What type of celebration is taking place on the ship, causing Ariel to swim to the surface and have her first encounter with Prince Eric?

5. Whom does Eric return to save when the great storm causes a fire on the ship?

6. What gift does Flounder present to Ariel in her secret underwater cavern?

7. Which character informs King Triton of Ariel's secret underwater cavern?

8. Which two despicable characters are the first to approach Ariel and inform her that Ursula may be able to help her?

9. Which character is the first to realize that the evil sea witch, Ursula, is in disguise, attempting to fool Prince Eric into thinking she is the one with the beautiful voice he remembered as his rescuer from drowning?

10. Who agrees to take the place of Ariel under the conditions of the contract she has signed with Ursula?

The Little Mermaid

Answers

1. A shark pursues Ariel and Flounder in one of the opening scenes. Fortunately, Ariel and Flounder prove too smart for the shark when they lead him to swim into the ring of an anchor.
2. King Triton has warned his daughter before, but this time he is quite serious when he instructs Ariel not to swim to the surface again. King Triton fears that his daughter will be seen by humans, whom he thinks are "barbarians."
3. Prince Eric calls Grimsby "old beanpole."
4. Ariel can only admire Eric from afar as she peeks in on his birthday celebration.
5. Eric goes back to the burning ship to save his dog, Max.
6. A stone statue of Prince Eric is in the grotto, and Flounder was the first to discover it and share it with Ariel. The statue was a present from Grimsby to Prince Eric for his birthday, but it was lost after the ship was destroyed.
7. Sebastian informs King Triton of the cavern.
8. Ursula's two eels, Flotsam and Jetsam, are the first to approach Ariel.
9. Scuttle accidentally flies near an open porthole on the ship and discovers the mysterious Vanessa is really Ursula in disguise.
10. King Triton agrees to take the place of his daughter in an effort to release Ariel from the conditions of the contract she has signed with Ursula.

Beauty and the Beast

November 22, 1991

Questions

1. According to the spell of the enchantress, until what year will the rose continue to bloom for the Beast?

2. Which character is the first to greet and welcome Maurice when he enters the Beast's castle after fleeing a pack of wolves?

3. Which actor provided the voice of the sinister proprietor of the local asylum?

4. Some comic relief is supplied during the film by three maidens seeking the affections of Gaston; what are their names?

5. What type of device has Maurice invented that he is convinced will win him first place at the fair?

6. According to Gaston and his song, what is he "especially good at"?

7. Which actress and actor supply the voices of the colorful Wardrobe and the town's gigolo, Gaston?

8. Which objects turn their heads to look at Belle during her guided tour of the castle?

9. What household positions are held by the characters Lumiere, Cogsworth, and Mrs. Potts in the Beast's castle?

10. Who saves Lumiere from the clutches of Le Fou after he and the townspeople invade the castle?

11. What color gown is worn by Belle during the ballroom scene?

12. Who makes himself into a stowaway when Belle returns to her cottage after saving her father?

13. How many total Academy Award nominations were received by the film *Beauty and the Beast*?

14. The character Belle makes a cameo appearance in what other full-length animated feature?

15. After the transformation of the Beast into the Prince, how does Belle first realize that he is the one she has fallen in love with?

Beauty and the Beast

Answers

1. According to the words and conditions of the spell, the enchanted rose will "bloom until the Prince's twenty-first year."
2. Lumiere.
3. The proprietor of the local asylum is Monsieur D'Arque, voiced by actor Tony Jay. Jay later provided the voice of the evil Judge Claude Frollo in *The Hunchback of Notre Dame* (1996).
4. They are known collectively and affectionately as the Bimbettes. In the Broadway stage show, they were known as the Silly Girls.
5. Maurice invented a device that successfully chops and stacks wood.
6. "I'm especially good at expectorating," proclaims Gaston.
7. Actress Jo Anne Worley provides the voice of Wardrobe and Broadway veteran Richard White supplies the voice of Gaston.
8. The suits of armor.
9. Lumiere is the butler, Cogsworth is the majordomo, and Mrs. Potts is the housekeeper.
10. Cogsworth.
11. Belle wears a gold gown.
12. Chip.
13. Six: three for Best Song, and one each for Best Sound, Best Musical Score, and Best Picture.
14. A careful look will reveal Belle in one of the crowd scenes of *The Hunchback of Notre Dame* (1996). In addition to Belle, the Magic Carpet from *Aladdin* (1992) and Pumbaa from *The Lion King* (1994) also make brief cameos.
15. When Belle looks into his eyes, she realizes he is the one.

Aladdin

November 25, 1992

Questions

1. Besides being a combination hookah and coffeemaker, what else does the device the narrator is offering for sale make?

2. Two townspeople say to each other, "On his way to the palace, I suppose" and "Another suitor for the princess." These two townspeople are actually caricatures of which two individuals?

3. Who is the first to say, "Only one may enter here. One whose worth lies far within. A diamond in the rough"?

4. What object from the Sultan must Jafar obtain in order to locate the right individual to enter the Cave of Wonders?

5. Which character from the film *Beauty and the Beast* (1991) makes a cameo appearance during the film *Aladdin*?

6. What song does the Genie first sing to Aladdin about his newfound wish potential?

7. What name does Aladdin assume when he becomes a Prince in order to impress Princess Jasmine?

8. Into what type of animal does the Genie transform Abu in order to help Aladdin?

9. According to the "Prince Ali" song, how many golden camels, purple peacocks, and white Persian monkeys does he have?

10. When Aladdin first arrives at the palace, which object is the Sultan fascinated with the most?

11. The Sultan's throne is shaped like what type of animal?

12. What is Jafar's official title when serving the Sultan?

13. How many different transformations did the Genie make during the film?

14. Which three individuals provided the inspiration for the development of the character Aladdin?

15. Actor Danny DeVito was originally suggested to provide the voice of which character in the film, *Aladdin*?

Aladdin

Answers

1. Besides being a combination hookah and coffeemaker, the device also makes julienne fries.
2. The two townspeople are actually caricatures of the film's directors, Ron Clements and John Musker.
3. The Tiger Head at the Cave of Wonders recites those words in reference to Aladdin.
4. Jafar must obtain the Sultan's Mystic Blue Diamond.
5. When the Sultan goes off to play with his toys, a small figurine of the Beast can be seen.
6. "Friend Like Me."
7. Aladdin is transformed into Prince Ali Ababwa in order to impress Princess Jasmine.
8. Abu, the monkey, becomes an elephant for Aladdin.
9. According to the song, he has seventy-five golden camels, fifty-three purple peacocks, and ninety-five white Persian monkeys.
10. The Sultan is fascinated with Aladdin's Magic Carpet.
11. The Sultan's throne is shaped like an elephant. Jafar's throne is in the shape of a cobra snake.
12. Jafar's official title is Royal Vizier, similar to a minister of state.
13. The Genie experienced a total of fifty-five transformations throughout the course of the film.
14. According to Glen Keane, the animator responsible for the development of the character, Aladdin's looks are fashioned after Tom Cruise's, his personality after Michael J. Fox's, and his clothing style was patterned after musical entertainer M. C. Hammer's.
15. Actor Danny DeVito was suggested to provide the voice of the parrot Iago. The part was written with him in mind, but he was unavailable for the role. DeVito did provide the voice of the character Philoctetes in *Hercules* (1997).

The Lion King

June 24, 1994

Questions

1. The Zulu expression chanted at the beginning of the film means what in English?

2. Which song from the film depicts the delicate balance of nature that binds all animals together?

3. In an effort to make the evil Scar stand out from the rest of the lion pride, what is different about his mane?

4. To what is Mufasa referring when he says to Simba, "Everything the light touches"?

5. When Mufasa teaches Simba about "pouncing," whom do they use as the unsuspecting recipient of their lesson?

6. Who saves Simba and Nala at the elephant graveyard from the three despicable hyenas, Shenzi, Banzai, and Ed?

7. What kind of animals are Timon and Pumbaa?

8. After Simba is rescued by Timon and Pumbaa, what song do the two teach him about their carefree lifestyle?

9. Which character from the Pride Lands is the first to realize Simba is still alive after having thought he was dead?

10. Who convinces Simba that he must return to the Pride Lands and regain the title of King rightfully due him?

11. What song does Zazu attempt to sing before being told by Scar, "No, no! Anything but that!?"

12. According to the law established by Scar, which individual's name is no one permitted to mention?

13. Which character joins Zazu while he is in the cage?

14. Which song from the film was almost edited out before singer Elton John insisted that it remain?

15. What do the Swahili names Simba, Pumbaa, and Rafiki mean?

The Lion King

Answers

1. "There's a lion, a very big lion!"
2. "Circle of Life."
3. Scar is the only lion with a black mane.
4. Mufasa is instructing his young son, Simba, about the boundaries of their kingdom.
5. Mufasa and Simba use Zazu as their unwilling participant during "pouncing lessons."
6. Mufasa himself saves Simba and Nala from the dangers of the three hyenas.
7. Timon is a meerkat and Pumbaa is a warthog.
8. The song title is "Hakuna Matata," which means "no worries" in English.
9. Nala is the first to realize Simba is still alive and can therefore recapture the title of King of the Pride Lands.
10. Rafiki reveals the image of Simba's father Mufasa to him. Rafiki then knocks some sense into Simba, making him realize the responsibility he must face at Pride Rock.
11. Zazu attempts to sing the song "It's a Small World."
12. According to the law established by Scar, no one is permitted to speak the name Mufasa.
13. Timon joins Zazu in the cage, seeking protection after being pursued by a group of hyenas.
14. "Can You Feel the Love Tonight."
15. Simba means "lion," Pumbaa means "dusty," and Rafiki means "friend."

Pocahontas

June 23, 1995

Questions

1. What is the name of Captain John Smith's ship and in what year is the film set?

2. The greedy Governor Ratcliffe thinks this new land will help fill his pockets with what precious commodity?

3. Which of Pocahontas's friends did animators originally conceive as a wild turkey?

4. What is the name of the little hummingbird that does not speak but is able to communicate with Pocahontas?

5. What is the name of the wise spirit found in an ancient tree at the Enchanted Glade, who counsels Pocahontas?

6. What is the name of the Indian warrior who asks for the hand of Pocahontas?

7. Besides biscuits, what other item does Meeko take from Captain John Smith's bag?

8. Which popular actor provides the voice of the legendary Captain John Smith?

9. In an effort to avoid even more bloodshed, whom does Captain John Smith save from a bullet fired by Governor Ratcliffe?

10. What color is not prominently used until one of the last sequences, when the Indians and settlers are about to battle?

Pocahontas

Answers

1. Captain John Smith sails the *Susan Constant* and the year is 1607.
2. Governor Ratcliffe thinks there is gold everywhere.
3. The mischievous little raccoon Meeko was originally going to be a wild turkey.
4. Flit.
5. The wise old tree is known as Grandmother Willow.
6. Kocoum asks for the hand of Pocahontas. Unfortunately, Kocoum is accidentally shot and killed by Thomas, one of the Jamestown settlers.
7. Meeko also takes Captain John Smith's compass.
8. Actor Mel Gibson supplies the voice of Captain John Smith.
9. Governor Ratcliffe intended to shoot the Indian tribe's leader and Pocahontas's father, Chief Powhatan. Captain John Smith is shot accidentally while saving Chief Powhatan.
10. The color red was not prominently used earlier in the film, so that the expected fight scene would be even more dramatic.

The Hunchback
of Notre Dame

June 21, 1996

Questions

1. Who is the only actor to supply a voice in each of the following full-length animated features: *Beauty and the Beast* (1991), *Pocahontas* (1995), and *The Hunchback of Notre Dame* (1996)?

2. How does Quasimodo receive his name and what does the name mean?

3. Who is the self-proclaimed leader of the Gypsies?

4. What are the names of the three gargoyles that befriend Quasimodo in the bell tower?

5. What is the name of the war hero who has returned to Paris and is appointed as Captain of the Guard by Judge Frollo?

6. What song does Quasimodo sing about his desire to be free and able to attend ceremonies such as the Festival of Fools?

7. Who is crowned the King of Topsy-Turvy Day during the Festival of Fools ceremony?

8. Why does Judge Frollo order the guards to seize and imprison Esmeralda?

9. What is the name of Esmeralda's pet goat?

10. After Esmeralda seeks sanctuary behind the cathedral's walls, who helps her to escape?

11. What is the name of the secret and legendary home of the Gypsies?

12. Who provides the voice of the characters Quasimodo and Esmeralda?

13. What is the original title of the 1831 novel that inspired the film, *The Hunchback of Notre Dame?*

14. Who provided the musical score for *The Hunchback of Notre Dame?*

15. Which city hosted the world premiere for *The Hunchback of Notre Dame?*

The Hunchback
of Notre Dame

Answers

1. David Ogden Stiers supplies the voice of Cogsworth and the narrator in *Beauty and the Beast* (1991), Governor Ratcliffe and Wiggins in *Pocahontas* (1995), and the Archdeacon in *The Hunchback of Notre Dame* (1996).
2. Judge Frollo gives him the name Quasimodo, which means "half-formed." Frollo is forced to care for Quasimodo as penance after causing the death of Quasimodo's mother when he was an infant.
3. Clopin.
4. Hugo, voiced by Jason Alexander; Victor, voiced by Charles Kimbrough; and Laverne, voiced by the late Mary Wickes.
5. Phoebus.
6. "Out There."
7. After the three gargoyles convince Quasimodo to attend the Festival of Fools, he is crowned King during the ceremony, much to the displeasure of his master, Judge Frollo.
8. First of all, Esmeralda is a Gypsy, and there is nothing Judge Frollo despises more. Secondly, Esmeralda defies Judge Frollo and talks back to him after she helps Quasimodo when the crowd becomes unruly.
9. The goat's name is Djali. The goat wears an earring in one ear, matching the one worn by Esmeralda.
10. Quasimodo helps Esmeralda to escape, allowing her the opportunity to return to her people.
11. The Court of Miracles.
12. Actor Tom Hulce, who may be best remembered for his title lead in the film *Amadeus* (1984), provides the voice of Quasimodo. Actress Demi Moore provides the speaking voice of the resourceful Esmeralda. Heidi Mollenhaver does the singing for Esmeralda.
13. The original title of Victor Hugo's 1831 novel is *Notre Dame de Paris*.
14. The Academy Award–winning team of Alan Menken and Stephen Schwartz. The pair originally teamed up for the film *Pocahontas* (1995).
15. New Orleans hosted the world premiere of *The Hunchback of Notre Dame* at the Superdome.

Hercules

June 27, 1997

Questions

1. What is the mythical home of the gods where Hercules was born?

2. Who kidnapped Hercules when he was a baby?

3. After Hercules visits the temple of Zeus, what makes him believe that his true place is not on Earth?

4. Whom does Hercules convince to come out of retirement and train him so he can become a hero?

5. What is the name of the beautiful but disillusioned young woman who captures the heart of Hercules?

Hercules

Answers

1. Mt. Olympus.
2. Hercules was kidnapped by two of Hades' evil minions, Pain and Panic. The two take the baby to Earth.
3. While at the temple the statue of Zeus comes to life and reveals to Hercules that he was originally a god on Olympus.
4. Philoctetes.
5. Megara.

Animated
Feature
Potpourri

....

Questions

1. In 1931, Walt Disney considered producing a film based on what classic story?

2. Which are the only two Disney films to be recognized for preservation by the Library of Congress?

3. Name the two previous Disney references to Jiminy Cricket prior to his introduction in the 1940 feature *Pinocchio*.

4. What country's film board determined that the film *Snow White and the Seven Dwarfs* (1937) was too scary for children, and those under sixteen must be accompanied by an adult?

5. In the films *Snow White and the Seven Dwarfs* (1937), *Cinderella* (1950), *Sleeping Beauty* (1959), and *The Little Mermaid* (1989), which is the only one to feature a prince with no name?

6. Which two characters are described in production notes as the "Janet Gaynor" and the "Douglas Fairbanks" type?

7. Who appeared on the cover of the December 27, 1937, issue of *Time* magazine?

8. Over the years which animated film has been released to theaters most often?

9. Which Disney full-length animated classic was originally released in only fourteen theaters throughout the world?

10. Which feature has been referred to as "Mickey's Mouse's *Citizen Kane*"?

11. Which full-length animated feature was the least expensive film to produce?

12. What full-length animated feature was based on a story by Helen Aberson and Harold Pearl?

13. What Academy Award did the feature *Dumbo* (1941) capture?

14. Not counting the film *Fantasia* (1940), which full-length animated feature has the least amount of dialogue?

15. Which is the first full-length animated feature to be released internationally before its United States release?

16. Which full-length animated feature was the shortest and which was the longest during their original premieres?

17. Which two Disney full-length animated features had Latin American releases prior to their United States releases?

18. Which full-length animated feature experienced the largest gap in time between its initial theater release and a subsequent rerelease?

19. In 1943 Walt Disney considered producing a film based on a book by a British airman. The story is about a collection of fantasy creatures who were responsible for the mechanical failures of airplanes. What was the feature's working title?

20. Which full-length animated feature includes the animated segments "Two Silhouettes" and "Without You"?

21. What animated segment from the feature *Make Mine Music* (1946) is based on an Ernest Lawrence Thayer poem that tells the story of a baseball player who was the "greatest, a giant, a tower of strength and a true pillar of his team"?

22. In the animated segment "Peter and the Wolf" from the 1946 feature *Make Mine Music*, each character is represented by a corresponding instrument in the orchestra. What musical instruments are used to represent Peter?

23. Which full-length animated feature stars the characters Joe and Jenny in a cartoon titled "Once Upon a Wintertime"?

24. Who provides the narration for the "Johnny Appleseed" animated segment from the feature *Melody Time* (1948)?

25. According to the legend, what kind of animals help raise Pecos Bill in the animated feature *Melody Time* (1948)?

26. Which full-length animated feature was originally dubbed *Two Fabulous Characters*?

27. What do the three characters J. Thaddeus Toad and Ichabod Crane from *The Adventures of Ichabod and Mr. Toad* (1949), and the White Rabbit from *Alice in Wonderland* (1951) all have in common?

28. What type of headgear is worn by Rat and Mole in the animated feature *The Adventures of Ichabod and Mr. Toad* (1949)?

29. Which 1950 full-length animated feature was based on the German story *Aschenputtel*?

30. Which animated feature's last line in the film is, "Well, come along. It's time for tea"?

31. Which are the only two full-length animated features to include mermaids?

32. Which feature includes the song "What Makes the Red Man Red?"

33. Which character from the feature *Peter Pan* (1953) makes a cameo appearance in the animated film *The Black Cauldron* (1985)?

34. Which actress provided the live-action model for the character Cruella De Vil in the 1961 animated classic *One Hundred and One Dalmatians?*

35. Which character from the feature *Lady and the Tramp* (1955) was originally referred to in production notes as Homer, Rags, and Bozo?

36. What is the title of the book written by author Miguel de Cervantes Saavedra, which was scheduled to serve as the inspiration for a proposed Disney full-length animated feature?

37. Which full-length animated feature includes the song "Skumps"?

38. Which feature includes a character named Diablo?

39. The puppy named Rolly, from *One Hundred and One Dalmatians* (1961) was referred to by what other name in the Dodie Smith book, on which the film is based?

40. Which is the only Disney full-length animated feature to be released on Christmas Day?

41. In the feature *The Sword in the Stone* (1963), how old is the character Arthur?

42. According to the song "Higitus Figitus" from *The Sword in the Stone* (1963), which items does the wizard Merlin pack first?

43. Which full-length animated feature was the first to be remade in a live-action version?

44. What was the only song in the feature *The Jungle Book* (1967) not written by the team of Richard and Robert Sherman?

45. About which Disney film can you make the statement, "The butler did it"?

46. In what year is the full-length animated feature *The Aristocats* (1970) set?

47. Which full-length animated film was the last to feature a storybook as part of its opening?

48. Which story was first released as a live-action film by Disney before being released as a full-length animated feature?

49. Which character from the feature *Robin Hood* (1973) was originally envisioned as a pig?

50. Which California university's well-known fight song can be heard in *Robin Hood?*

51. Which song from the film *Pinocchio* (1940) was featured in *Close Encounters of the Third Kind* (1977) from Columbia Pictures?

52. Which character is described in a song as "willy nilly silly ole bear"?

53. The author who penned the Pooh stories gained his inspiration by watching whom?

54. What contribution did Ernest H. Shepard make to the *Winnie the Pooh* stories?

55. Name the first full-length animated features to be released on video and the year of their release.

56. Who wrote the song "Best of Friends" from the full-length animated feature *The Fox and the Hound* (1981)?

57. Which is the only full-length animated classic not to include any songs?

58. Which author wrote the stories on which *The Black Cauldron* (1985) is based?

59. What foreign country has provided the setting for the most full-length animated features?

60. What character sings the song "The World's Greatest Criminal Mind"?

61. During the 1992 Academy Awards broadcast, which animated character made a cameo appearance?

62. Besides their appearance in *Fantasia* (1940), the two characters Mlle. Upanova and Hyacinth Hippo also made a cameo in what other film?

63. Which full-length animated feature was the first one to produce a theatrical sequel?

64. Name the five full-length animated features to be based on classic fairy tales.

65. Which full-length animated feature was the first to be produced as a stage show in a Disney theme park while it simultaneously ran in theaters?

66. Which film did Warner Brothers animator Chuck Jones refer to as "the funniest feature ever made?"

67. Which was the first full-length animated feature to receive a Golden Globe nomination for Best Actor?

68. Popular lyricist Tim Rice, whose Disney theatrical credits include *The Lion King* (1994) and *Aladdin* (1992), played in what early 1960s musical group?

69. Which full-length animated feature was the first to be completely computer digitized before it was rereleased to theaters?

70. What was the first full-length animated feature to be translated into the Zulu language?

71. Which full-length animated feature held its world premiere before the largest audience ever?

72. Which was the first full-length animated feature to be based on historical events and people?

73. Name the eight full-length Disney animated features whose titles are composed of only a single word.

74. Which classic story series by author Edgar Rice Burroughs provides the inspiration for a future full-length animated feature?

Animated Feature Potpourri

Answers

1. In 1931, Walt Disney wanted to produce a film based on Lewis Carroll's *Alice in Wonderland*. Walt decided to shelve the project after Commonwealth Pictures Corporation made their own version of the Lewis Carroll classic. Walt Disney finally released his own animated version of *Alice in Wonderland* in 1951.

2. *Snow White and the Seven Dwarfs* (1937) and *Fantasia* (1940).

3. In *Snow White and the Seven Dwarfs* (1937), the Dwarfs utter the exclamation "jiminy crickets" when they realize a stranger is in their cottage. The exclamation was also made in the classic animated short *Brave Little Tailor* (1938).

4. England.

5. Snow White's prince is simply known as "the Prince," while Cinderella had her Prince Charming, Aurora had Prince Phillip, and Ariel had Prince Eric.

6. Snow White was referred to in production notes as the "Janet Gaynor" type and the Prince, from the same feature, was described as the "Douglas Fairbanks" type.

7. Walt Disney appeared on the December 27, 1937, issue of *Time* magazine, along with models of the Dwarfs from *Snow White and the Seven Dwarfs*. The film itself had its world premiere just six days before the date of issue.

8. *Snow White and the Seven Dwarfs* (1937) has appeared in theaters more than any other animated feature. Over the years, the film, including its initial debut, has appeared in theaters a total of nine times.

9. *Fantasia* (1940) ran in only fourteen theaters during its original release. The reason was that the film's complicated sound system was expensive and parts were in short supply due to war preparations.

10. *Fantasia* (1940), for Mickey's portrayal in the musical segment *The Sorcerer's Apprentice*.

11. At a cost of $812,000, *Dumbo* (1941) was the least expensive feature to produce.

12. *Dumbo* (1941).

13. *Dumbo* won the Academy Award for Best Score.

14. *Bambi* (1942), which includes approximately eight hundred words.

15. *Bambi* was released first in London on August 13, 1942. On August 21, 1942, the film was released in the United States at Radio City Music Hall in New York.

16. *Saludos Amigos* (1943) was the shortest feature running only 42 minutes, and *Fantasia* (1940) was the longest, running 125 minutes.

17. The two features were *Saludos Amigos* (1943) and *The Three Caballeros* (1945). The south-of-the-border releases each occurred during the year previous to their U.S. release.

18. *The Three Caballeros,* was originally released to theaters in 1945, and was not released again until 1977.

19. The working title for the feature was *The Gremlins*. The author and British airman who penned the work was Roald Dahl. Another book by Dahl was eventually produced by Disney as a film in 1996, titled *James and the Giant Peach*. In addition, Dahl's book *Charlie and the Chocolate Factory* became the inspiration for the non-Disney film *Willy Wonka and the Chocolate Factory* (1971).

20. They represent two of the ten animated segments in the 1946 full-length animated feature *Make Mine Music.*

21. "Casey at the Bat."

22. Peter is represented by a string quartet. Among the other characters, the cat is represented by a clarinet, the bird by a flute, the duck by an oboe, and the hunters by kettle drums.

23. "Once Upon a Wintertime" is one of seven animated segments that make up the 1948 feature *Melody Time.*

24. Dennis Day tells the story of the settler Johnny Appleseed, who headed west and planted apple trees along his journey.

25. A family of coyotes helped raise Pecos Bill.

26. During production, *The Adventures of Ichabod and Mr. Toad* (1949) was originally dubbed *Two Fabulous Characters.*

27. J. Thaddeus Toad, Ichabod Crane, and White Rabbit all have "Esq." appended to their names.

28. Rat wears a deerstalker, a hat similar to the one worn by famed detective Sherlock Holmes. Mole dons a bowler. Basil Rathbone, who portrayed Sherlock Holmes in many films, serves as the narrator for the "Mr. Toad" segment of *The Adventures of Ichabod and Mr. Toad* (1949).

29. *Cinderella* was first recorded in German literature during the sixteenth century. The title, "Aschenputtel," means "little cinder girl."

30. *Alice in Wonderland* (1951).

31. The first appearance of mermaids was in *Peter Pan* (1953) and the second was, of course, *The Little Mermaid* (1989).
32. *Peter Pan* (1953).
33. Tinker Bell makes a cameo appearance in the land of the Fair Folk.
34. Mary Wickes.
35. The character Tramp was referred to in production notes by the names Homer, Rags, and Bozo before the name Tramp was chosen. The Siamese cats, Si and Am, were originally called Nip and Tuck.
36. *Don Quijote de La Mancha* was suggested as a full-length animated feature; the project was shelved, however. Some early concept art was done for the film.
37. *Sleeping Beauty* (1959).
38. Diablo is the name of Maleficent's sinister pet raven in the feature *Sleeping Beauty* (1959).
39. In the Dodie Smith book, *One Hundred and One Dalmatians,* the puppy that is always hungry was known as Roly Poly.
40. *The Sword in the Stone* was released on December 25, 1963.
41. Arthur, whose nickname is Wart, is eleven when he meets the wizard Merlin. His voice is provided by two actors, Ricky Sorenson and Robert Reitherman, the son of the film's director, Wolfgang Reitherman.
42. Merlin packs his books first.
43. In 1967, Disney released a full-length animated feature based on Rudyard Kipling's *The Jungle Book.* In 1994, a live-action version of the film was released.
44. The Sherman brothers were responsible for the entire musical score except for the song "The Bare Necessities." The song was written by Terry Gilkyson. One song, titled "The Land of Sand," was written for the film but never used.
45. In the film *The Aristocats* (1970), the villain is the butler Edgar.
46. *The Aristocats* is set in Paris in 1910.
47. *Robin Hood* (1973) was the last film to begin with a storybook that opens, a common practice for Disney features, beginning with *Snow White and the Seven Dwarfs* (1937).
48. *The Story of Robin Hood and His Merrie Men* was released in 1952 as a live-action film by Disney and then the story served as the basis for a full-length animated feature in 1973, titled *Robin Hood.*
49. The character Friar Tuck was originally envisioned as a pig.
50. The fight song from the University of Southern California (USC) can be heard in the feature *Robin Hood.*

51. "When You Wish Upon a Star."
52. Winnie the Pooh.
53. The inspiration for Pooh came to author A. A. Milne after observing his five-year-old son, Christopher Robin, playing with his stuffed animals and identifying the strong relationship he had with them.
54. Ernest H. Shepard was the original illustrator of the A. A. Milne *Winnie the Pooh* stories.
55. In June of 1981, *Dumbo* (1941) and *The Many Adventures of Winnie the Pooh* (1977) were released on video. In October of that same year, *Alice in Wonderland* (1951) was also released.
56. The song "Best of Friends" was written by Stan Fidel and Richard Johnston, the latter the son of legendary animator Ollie Johnston.
57. *The Black Cauldron* (1985).
58. Lloyd Alexander's five-volume mythological fantasy titled *The Chronicles of Prydain* (1964–68) inspired the film *The Black Cauldron*.
59. England has provided the setting for more full-length animated features than any other country.
60. The villain Ratigan, from the full-length animated feature *The Great Mouse Detective* (1986)
61. In honor of her fifty-fifth anniversary, Snow White appeared in animated form.
62. Both characters who starred in the *Fantasia* (1940) musical segment "Dance of the Hours" made cameo appearances in the film *Who Framed Roger Rabbit* (1988).
63. *The Rescuers* was released in 1977; its sequel, *The Rescuers Down Under,* was released in 1990.
64. *Snow White and the Seven Dwarfs* (1937), *Cinderella* (1950), *Sleeping Beauty* (1959), *The Little Mermaid* (1989), and *Beauty and the Beast* (1991) are the only five based on classic fairy tales.
65. Disneyland and Disney-MGM Studios both presented stage versions of *Beauty and the Beast* while the film itself ran in theaters.
66. Animator Chuck Jones, who is best known for his work with "Bugs Bunny" and "Roadrunner" cartoons, referred to the 1992 film *Aladdin* as "the funniest feature ever made."
67. Robin Williams was nominated for his portrayal of the Genie in the 1992 feature *Aladdin.*
68. Tim Rice was a member of the rock band The Aardvarks from 1961 to 1963.
69. For its 1993 reissue, *Snow White and the Seven Dwarfs* was cleaned up and completely digitized by computer.

70. *The Lion King* (1994).
71. *Pocahontas* held its world premiere on June 10, 1995, at New York's Central Park in front of an estimated audience of two hundred thousand. The film was shown on a collection of four large screens.
72. *Pocahontas* (1995).
73. *Pinocchio* (1940), *Fantasia* (1940), *Dumbo* (1941), *Bambi* (1942), *Cinderella* (1950), *Aladdin* (1992), *Pocahontas* (1995), and *Hercules* (1997).
74. *Tarzan*.

Disney on Television

Questions

1. What was the title of the first episode to air on the television program *Disneyland?*

2. Walt Disney received an Emmy Award in 1955 and in 1956. In what two categories did Walt Disney receive the awards?

3. What was the first Disney television miniseries to be released theatrically?

4. Which character is known as the one who "patched up the crack in the Liberty Bell"?

5. In 1955 Walt Disney lost what special recognition and award to television personality George Gobel?

6. In *Davy Crockett's Keelboat Race* (1955) what are the names of the keelboats featured in the race?

7. Complete the line from this song: "Out of the night, when the full moon is bright, comes a horseman known as"—who?

8. What Disney television program was the first to incorporate the use of sign language?

9. What is the name of Zorro's father in the series?

10. What is the title of the short-lived Disney television sequel to *Zorro?*

11. Famous German rocket scientist Wernher von Braun and animator Ward Kimball worked together to create what celebrated television show?

12. What is the title of the perennial Christmas special, first aired in 1958 and hosted by Jiminy Cricket?

13. Which television hero is best known for the expression "Made 'em do what they oughter"?

14. Which popular 1959 Disney film was originally intended for television audiences?

15. Which television network owned a percentage of Disneyland park when it opened?

16. In what year did Walt Disney's long-running television program move to its familiar Sunday night time slot?

17. Which animated character made his debut not in a theatrical cartoon but on the first Disney color television show?

18. Before Mickey Mouse starred in the 1990 version of *The Prince and the Pauper,* a three-part miniseries was broadcast in 1962. Who played the title roles in this live-action version?

19. Which actor and Disney regular starred in the 1962 television show *The Mooncussers* as well as in the 1963 show *Johnny Shiloh?*

20. How many Emmy Awards were personally won by Walt Disney and his Studios during his lifetime?

21. What is the name of the 1967 three-part miniseries starring Kurt Russell in the role of the young rebel soldier during the American Civil War?

22. Which 1970 full-length animated feature was originally planned to be a two-part live-action special on television?

23. Which Disney television series was the first to go into syndication?

24. Which actresses starred in the 1982 television show *The Adventures of Pollyanna?*

25. Which 1969 Disney film provided the inspiration for a short-lived television sequel in 1982?

26. What is the name of The Disney Channel series hosted by author George Plimpton?

27. What is the name of The Disney Channel series featuring the characters The Ringmaster, Sebastian, and Fair Dinkum?

28. What is the name of The Disney Channel live-action series devoted to Winnie the Pooh and his friends?

29. What is the name of The Disney Channel series about a marine biologist and his family and their life in the Pacific Northwest?

30. What is the name of The Disney Channel series that details the plight of a group of Americans and Australians who work together to establish a stage post in the hostile Australian Outback during the Gold Rush days?

31. In 1988 Disney released a television special titled *Disney's Magic in the Magic Kingdom.* During the special an illusion was created that caused the castle in Disneyland to disappear. Which popular team of illusionists accomplished this impossible task?

32. What is the name of the Weston family's bothersome neighbor on the Touchstone television series *Empty Nest?*

33. The television series *Empty Nest* was a spin-off of which other television program?

34. Which character from the animated cartoon series *Chip an' Dale's Rescue Rangers* is named after a type of cheese?

35. Which character from an animated cartoon series is best known for his expression "Let's get dangerous!"?

36. Which character from a television series is best remembered for the phrase "Gotta love me!"?

37. What city provides the setting for the television series *Home Improvement?*

38. What is the name of the fictitious tool company that provides the sponsorship for Tim Taylor's show within a show on *Home Improvement?*

39. On the television series *Home Improvement,* Tim and Jill Taylor have three children; what are their names?

40. To date, which Disney television program has captured the most Emmy Awards?

41. Which actor starred in The Disney Channel release *Mark Twain and Me?*

42. What is the name of The Disney Channel original program that features an android named Chip, and stars Jay Underwood and Alan Thicke?

43. What is Goofy's profession on the animated cartoon series *Goof Troop?*

44. In the animated cartoon series *Goof Troop,* what are the names of Pete's two children?

45. What is the name of Pete's vicious dog in *Goof Troop?*

46. Rider Strong and Will Friedle are supporting players in which Disney television series?

47. What city provides the setting for the television series *Boy Meets World?*

48. What does the character George Hamilton Feeny portray on the television series *Boy Meets World?*

49. What is the name of the first show ever to run commercially as well as on the Public Broadcasting Service simultaneously?

50. What is the name of the short-lived Touchstone television series starring Henry Winkler playing the role of a conservative talk show host?

51. What was the original name for the Touchstone television series *Ellen?*

52. Actress Ellen DeGeneres, star of the series *Ellen*, earlier appeared as a regular on what short-lived Touchstone television program?

53. What type of business is run by Ellen Morgan in *Ellen?*

54. A recurring character on the series *Ellen* is her mother. What does Ellen's mother want her daughter to do more than anything?

55. Which stand-up comedian starred in the Touchstone television series *All-American Girl?*

56. What is the name of the short-lived Disney television program about a screwball baseball team and the escapades of their season?

57. What is the name of the first dramatic animated cartoon series to be produced by Disney?

58. What is the name of the mysterious castle guarded by the legendary gargoyles in the animated cartoon series by that same name?

59. What country provides the original setting for *Gargoyles* and the castle they are sworn to protect?

60. What are the terms of the spell cast upon the gargoyles by Megasis, the Princess's adviser, in the year A.D. 994?

61. What is the name of the greedy businessman who learns the secret of the gargoyles, brings them to New York city, places the castle they protect atop a giant skyscraper, and looks to exploit their power for his own benefit?

62. Actor Ed Asner, star of the Touchstone television program *Thunder Alley,* provides the voice of which warrior in the animated cartoon series *Gargoyles?*

63. Who is the leader of the powerful gargoyles?

64. By nature, gargoyles are protective. What is the name of the evil gargoyle that defies all that they stand for?

65. What is the name of the police detective who originally befriends the gargoyles and attempts to teach them the ways of the twentieth century?

66. What are the names of the three Lawrence brothers that star in the series *Brotherly Love?*

67. What actress has played the same feisty character on five live-action Disney television series?

68. Which star from a 1991 full-length animated feature appears in her own live-action television show?

69. Which short-lived Touchstone television series tells the story of two young filmmakers struggling to make ends meet in Chicago?

70. What is the name of the animated cartoon series about a team of hockey-playing superheroes from a parallel universe?

71. What is Donald and Daisy's profession in the animated cartoon series *Quack Pack?*

72. Which trio once again appears, this time in the animated cartoon series *Quack Pack,* to cause Donald all types of grief?

73. Which 1961 full-length animated feature serves as the inspiration and storyline for an animated cartoon series?

74. Mowgli, Baloo, and Bagheera are just some of the stars from the 1967 full-length animated feature *The Jungle Book* who return in their own animated cartoon series. What is the name of this cartoon series?

75. Beginning in 1954 with the television program *Disneyland,* up to its most recent series, how many different titles has Disney's weekly anthology show had over the years?

Disney
on Television

Answers

1. *The Disneyland Story,* also known as *What Is Disneyland?* (1954).
2. In 1955 Walt Disney received an Emmy Award for Best Variety Series and in 1956 he received the award for Best Producer of Filmed Series both for *Disneyland.*
3. The three-part miniseries featuring Davy Crockett, which first aired in 1954 on the television program *Disneyland,* was the first to be released theatrically. The theater release was titled *Davy Crockett, King of the Wild Frontier.*
4. The line describes the legendary figure Davy Crockett, and is from the song *The Ballad of Davy Crockett.*
5. After his first season on television, Walt Disney was nominated for an Emmy Award as Most Outstanding New Personality, but the recognition and award went to George Gobel.
6. Davy Crockett's keelboat is known as the *Bertha Mae* and Mike Fink sailed the *Gullywhumper.*
7. Zorro.
8. The character Bernardo used a form of sign language in *Zorro.*
9. Zorro's father is Don Alejandro, played by actor George Lewis. Lewis played the role of Zorro himself in an earlier serial produced by Republic.
10. The series was called *Zorro and Son* (1983) and was composed of five episodes.
11. The two worked together to create the successful show *Man in Space* (1955). The show depicted a fascinating survey of space travel past, present, and future. According to reports, the show was so popular it helped provide an impetus to government officials who were beginning development of the U.S. space program.
12. *From All of Us to All of You.*
13. Television hero and lawman Texas John Slaughter.
14. Walt Disney had devised the 1959 feature *The Shaggy Dog* for television but deemed it of high enough quality to be worthy of a theatrical release instead. Fortunately for Disney, the theatrical release of *The Shaggy Dog* did prove to be successful. The film was the top box office hit of 1959.
15. The American Broadcasting Company (ABC), a company now owned

by The Walt Disney Company, owned 34.48 percent of Disneyland park up to the year 1960.

16. Beginning with the 1960–61 television season, the show moved to its familiar Sunday night time slot. Prior to that year the series aired on Wednesday and later on Friday nights.

17. Donald Duck's eccentric uncle, Ludwig Von Drake.

18. Sean Scully starred in the live-action version of *The Prince and the Pauper.*

19. Kevin Corcoran.

20. Walt Disney and his staff captured a total of seven Emmy Awards during his lifetime.

21. *Willie and the Yank.* The foreign theatrical title was *Mosby's Marauders.*

22. *The Aristocats* (1970).

23. The original *Mickey Mouse Club* series was the first to go into television syndication.

24. Shirley Jones and Patsy Kensit.

25. *The Love Bug* (1969) provided the inspiration for the five-episode television series *Herbie, the Love Bug,* which aired in 1982.

26. *Mouseterpiece Theatre.*

27. *Dumbo's Circus.*

28. *Welcome to Pooh Corner.*

29. *Danger Bay.*

30. *Five-Mile Creek.* A young Nicole Kidman is featured as one of the stars.

31. The team of Siegfried & Roy.

32. Charley Dietz.

33. *The Golden Girls.*

34. Monterey Jack.

35. Darkwing Duck.

36. Baby Sinclair from the television series *Dinosaurs.*

37. Detroit, Michigan, provides the backdrop for the Touchstone series *Home Improvement.*

38. Binford Tools.

39. Brad, Randy, and Mark.

40. From 1985 through 1992 the Touchstone television series *The Golden Girls* captured a total of eleven Emmy Awards, more than any other single Disney program.

41. Jason Robards.

42. *Not Quite Human.*

43. Goofy works as a photographer, specializing in children's portraits.

44. Pete has two children; a son named P.J. and a daughter named Pistol. The actress who supplies the voice of the character Pistol is Nancy

Cartwright. Cartwright also has the task of providing the voice of Bart Simpson on Fox's *The Simpsons.*

45. Appropriately, Pete's dog is named Chainsaw.
46. *Boy Meets World.*
47. Philadelphia.
48. George Hamilton Feeny, played by actor William Daniels, is the principal. He was a teacher during the first season.
49. *Disney Presents Bill Nye the Science Guy.*
50. *Monty.*
51. When the series *Ellen* earlier aired it was known as *These Friends of Mine.*
52. Ellen DeGeneres played the quick-witted registered nurse Nancy MacIntyre on the Touchstone series *Laurie Hill.*
53. Ellen runs a bookstore, which has the clever name Buy the Book.
54. It seems, no matter what the conversation's topic may be, Ellen's mother keeps emphasizing that her daughter should find someone nice and get married.
55. Margaret Cho.
56. *Hardball.*
57. *Gargoyles.*
58. Castle Wivern.
59. Scotland.
60. According to the spell, gargoyles will "sleep until the castle rises above the clouds."
61. David Xanatos, voiced by actor Jonathan Frakes, is the greedy businessman. Frakes may be best known for his portrayal of William T. Riker on the long-running television series *Star Trek: The Next Generation.*
62. Ed Asner supplies the voice of Hudson.
63. Goliath is the mighty leader of the gargoyles, voiced by Keith David.
64. Demona, voiced by actress Marina Sirtis, is the evil gargoyle. Sirtis herself may be best known for her portrayal of Counselor Troi on the long-running television series *Star Trek: The Next Generation.*
65. The New York City detective is Elisa Maza, voiced by Salli Richardson.
66. Joey, Matthew, and Andrew Lawrence.
67. Estelle Getty portrayed the character Sophia Petrillo on five live-action series.
68. Belle from the 1991 feature *Beauty and the Beast* stars in the television series *Disney's Sing Me a Story: With Belle.*
69. *Buddies.*

70. *Disney's The Mighty Ducks.*
71. In the animated cartoon series *Quack Pack*, Donald, who goes by the name Don, is a cameraman and Daisy is a reporter for a television entertainment–news show called *What In the World.*
72. Donald's three nephews Huey, Dewey, and Louie return in the series *Quack Pack.* This time around the three appear as teenagers.
73. The stars from the 1961 film *One Hundred and One Dalmatians* appear in their own animated cartoon series in the 1997 television line-up.
74. The series features them as youngsters and is called *Jungle Cubs.*
75. A total of eight different names have been used over the years: *Disneyland* (1954–58), *Walt Disney Presents* (1958–61), *Walt Disney's Wonderful World of Color* (1961–69), *The Wonderful World of Disney* (1969–79), *Disney's Wonderful World* (1979–81), *Walt Disney* (1981–83), *The Disney Sunday Movie* (1986–88), and *The Magical World of Disney* (1988–90).

Mickey Mouse Club

....

Questions

1. What popular *Mickey Mouse Club* song includes the words "Meeska! Mooska! Mouseketeer!"?

2. Which two Mouseketeers were occasionally referred to as Meeseketeers because they represented two of the youngest and smallest of the original Mouseketeers?

3. Which individual has been credited for suggesting the Mickey Mouse ears worn by the Mouseketeers for the show?

4. Which animated character is the first to trumpet "M-O-U-S-E" for the opening of each show on the original *Mickey Mouse Club* series?

5. Which *Mickey Mouse Club* song opens with the words "Saddle your pony, here we go!"?

6. On the original series, who was the last individual to give his name for the *Mickey Mouse Club* roll call?

7. During its first season, was the original *Mickey Mouse Club* series on for an hour or a half hour?

8. At the time of the debut of the *Mickey Mouse Club* series the popular mouse ears, like those worn by the Mouseketeers, were made available for sale; how much did they originally sell for?

9. Which two individuals served as producer and director of the original *Mickey Mouse Club* series?

10. Which famous entertainer's two sons were cast as original Mouseketeers?

11. Which animated character is known for his "I'm no fool" philosophy on the *Mickey Mouse Club* series?

12. Which actress played the society girl who was jealous of the beauty, popularity, and talent possessed by the country girl, Annette, on the *Mickey Mouse Club* serial *Annette?*

13. Who played Annette's boyfriend on *Annette?*

14. What is the name of the *Mickey Mouse Club* serial about two boys, one American and one British, who team up to outwit a band of criminals?

15. What are the names of the horses ridden by Spin and Marty on the *Mickey Mouse Club* serial *The Adventures of Spin and Marty?*

16. What is the name of the rival camp on *The Adventures of Spin and Marty?*

17. What role does the character Perkins play on *The Adventures of Spin and Marty?*

18. In an effort to resolve their differences, Spin and Marty square off in a boxing match; which of the two boys wins the fight?

19. Which popular Western movie actor played the role of camp counselor Bill on *The Adventures of Spin and Marty?*

20. Which Mouseketeer asked Walt Disney one day if she should change her last name to Turner because everyone had been mispronouncing her real name?

21. Which Mouseketeer went on to portray Chuck Conners's son on the television program *The Rifleman?*

22. Which Mouseketeer played the character Alice for the 1958

official grand opening of the Disneyland attraction Alice in Wonderland?

23. Which Mouseketeer recorded songs for the musical album *Sleeping Beauty?*

24. Which Mouseketeer became a regular on the long-running television program *The Lawrence Welk Show?*

25. Which original Mouseketeer later served as a drummer for the musical group The Carpenters?

26. Which original Mouseketeer later won an Emmy Award for Best Makeup for his work on the acclaimed miniseries *Backstairs at the White House?*

27. Which Disney regular from the original *Mickey Mouse Club* series served as one of the producers for the long-running television program *Murder, She Wrote,* starring Angela Lansbury?

28. Which Mouseketeer was honored in 1993 with her own star on the Hollywood Walk of Fame?

29. Which two Mouseketeers from the 1977 *Mickey Mouse Club* series went on to star in the long-running television program *The Facts of Life?*

30. On the new updated *Mickey Mouse Club* series, which actor who later starred in the television program *Beverly Hills 90210* starred in the serial *Teen Angel?*

Mickey Mouse Club

Answers

1. The official title of the song is "Mousekartoon Time." The song helped introduce that show's selected Disney animated cartoon.
2. The two Meeseketeers were Carl "Cubby" O'Brien and Karen Pendleton.
3. Roy Williams. Williams was an animator and storyman with the Disney Studios before being selected to participate in the original *Mickey Mouse Club* series. According to the story, Williams got his inspiration for the mouse ears from the non-Disney character Felix the Cat, who would occasionally lift his own ears off from the top of his head as a cartoon prank.
4. Dumbo.
5. The song "Talent Round-up."
6. Jimmie Dodd was the last to give his name for the *Mickey Mouse Club* roll call. Dodd served as the head Mouseketeer.
7. During its first season, the *Mickey Mouse Club* was on for an hour.
8. They sold for sixty-nine cents and were manufactured by the Benay-Albee Novelty Co. of Maspeth, New York.
9. Sidney Miller served as the director and Bill Walsh acted as producer for the series.
10. Mickey Rooney's two sons, Mickey Jr. and Tim Rooney, were selected as original Mouseketeers but they appeared in only a few episodes.
11. Jiminy Cricket is known for his "I'm no fool" philosophy on the *Mickey Mouse Club* series.
12. Roberta Shore was the society girl on *Annette*.
13. Disney regular Tim Considine played Annette's boyfriend.
14. *The Adventures of Clint and Mac,* starring Jonathan Bailey and Neil Wolfe.
15. Spin rode a horse named Sailor and Marty rode Skyrocket. Marty initially had a fear of horses, but by riding Skyrocket he was able to conquer his fear.
16. The rival camp is known as North Fork.
17. Perkins, played by popular Disney voice actor J. Pat O'Malley, is the manservant of the rich, spoiled Marty.
18. The boxing match between Spin and Marty was officially declared a draw.

19. Veteran actor Harry Carey, Jr. played camp counselor Bill. In the series, Roy Barcroft played the role of the camp leader.

20. Annette Funicello wanted to change her last name to Turner because everyone was mispronouncing her real name. Walt Disney encouraged Annette to retain her last name, which she did. Walt said she had a beautiful last name and "once people learn how to pronounce it, they will never forget it."

21. Mouseketeer Johnny Crawford became the son of Chuck Conners on *The Rifleman.*

22. Karen Pendleton.

23. Darlene Gillespie.

24. Mouseketeer Bobby Burgess was a regular on *The Lawrence Welk Show* for more than seventeen years.

25. Mouseketeer Carl "Cubby" O'Brien.

26. Tommy Cole.

27. Kevin Corcoran.

28. Annette Funicello.

29. Mindy Feldman and Lisa Whelchel played the characters Natalie and Blair on *The Facts of Life.*

30. Jason Priestley.

Live-Action Films

Walt Disney Pictures

Questions

1. Which rarely seen feature includes "Song of the Eagle?"

2. Which was the first completely live-action Disney feature filmed solely in the United States?

3. Which was the first live-action feature filmed at the Walt Disney Studios in Burbank, California?

4. Which was the only Disney feature film to have a Revolutionary War setting?

5. What is the name of the Academy Award–winning Disney matte artist and special effects master whose projects include *Treasure Island* (1950), *20,000 Leagues Under the Sea* (1954), *Darby O'Gill and the Little People* (1959), and *Mary Poppins* (1964), to name just a few?

6. Which film was inspired after Walt Disney apparently saw an experiment involving carbon dioxide gas?

7. Name the three films released by Walt Disney Pictures that were produced in black and white.

8. In addition to appearing in the 1963 full-length animated feature *The Sword in the Stone*, the characters Arthur and Merlin were in which two later Disney films?

9. Which country provides the setting for the 1963 film *The Three Lives of Thomasina*?

10. Which famous silent film star appeared in the film *The Moon-Spinners* (1964)?

11. What song from the film *Mary Poppins* (1964) did Walt Disney believe would become so popular that it would replace the *Brahms Lullaby*?

12. When Mary Poppins takes the job of the Banks family's new nanny, what two requirements does she place on her employment?

13. Which song from *Mary Poppins* received its inspiration from the pub song "Knees Up, Mother Brown?"

14. Which Academy Award–winning actress portrayed the role of the old birdwoman in *Mary Poppins*?

15. Which 1965 film is about a New England trapper who dreams of building a sanctuary for migrating birds?

16. Award-winning television actor Tom Skerritt made his theatrical screen debut in which 1965 Disney film?

17. Actors Rex Harrison, Brian Keith, and Burt Lancaster were all considered for a role in which film before the part was given eventually to Fred MacMurray?

18. Which 1967 film is based on the book, *My Philadelphia Father*?

19. What is the name of the Christmas ballad sung by Fred MacMurray and Greer Garson for the 1967 film *The Happiest Millionaire*?

20. The song "A Step in the Right Direction" was dropped from what film's final version?

21. Which film stars James Garner as an Army deserter who flees to Mexico with two stolen camels?

22. Actor Michael J. Fox made his screen debut in which 1980 Disney film?

23. Name the 1983 film about a mystery writer who, while vacationing in Malta, becomes caught up in her own true-life mystery.

24. What famous play provided the inspiration for the film *Something Wicked This Way Comes* (1983)?

25. What type of carnival ride makes people younger when run in reverse in the film, *Something Wicked This Way Comes*?

26. Which Disney film has a character named Beauty who is actually a villain?

27. Which film includes characters named Sanka Coffie, Yul Brenner, Junior Bevil, and Derice Bannock?

28. What object does one of the bobsledders place under his helmet for good luck in the film *Cool Runnings* (1994)?

29. What is the name of the coach in the film *Cool Runnings*, whose philosophy concerning the Olympic Gold Medal is, "If you're not enough without it, you'll never be enough with it!"

30. The song "All for Love" appeared in which 1993 Disney film?

31. Which two cities provide the setting for the race in the film *Iron Will* (1994)?

32. In the film *Blank Check* (1994), what amount does Preston Waters write on the check he received for his damaged bicycle?

33. The Ducks are asked to represent the United States during what competition in *D2: The Mighty Ducks* (1994)?

34. What country do the Ducks face off against during the championship game in *D2: The Mighty Ducks*?

35. Besides the 1994 full-length animated feature *The Lion King*, which two other Disney films include the phrase "hakuna matata"?

36. The film *Angels in the Outfield* (1994) held its world premiere at what facility?

37. During a game, what gesture does Roger make whenever he sees an angel in the 1994 film *Angels in the Outfield*?

38. Which 1994 film tells the tale of a legendary native American who lived in New England in the 1600s and befriended the early Pilgrims?

39. What does the "clause" actually stipulate on the business card in the film *The Santa Clause* (1994)?

40. In *The Santa Clause*, what does the head elf, Bernard, give to Scott's son, Charlie, so that he will always remember his father and know that he is always close?

41. In the live-action version of *The Jungle Book* (1994), what is the name of Mowgli's girlfriend and what object did she present to him when the two were very young?

42. Which film set in Elma, Texas, tells the story of a British schoolteacher and her efforts to unite the town by organizing a children's soccer team?

43. Which 1995 documentary features the history of two legendary Disney animators in the very early days of animation?

44. Which two films include a character named Bo Peep?

45. Which character from the 1995 feature *Toy Story*, is associated with the phrase "To infinity and beyond?"

46. The feature *Toy Story* (1995) represents a true buddy film. Which two popular actors provide the voices of Buzz Lightyear and Cowboy Woody?

47. What happens to the contents of the bag that sets James out on his incredible journey in the film *James and the Giant Peach* (1996)?

48. The character Jack Skellington, star of the 1993 film *Tim Burton's The Nightmare Before Christmas* made a cameo appearance in which 1996 feature?

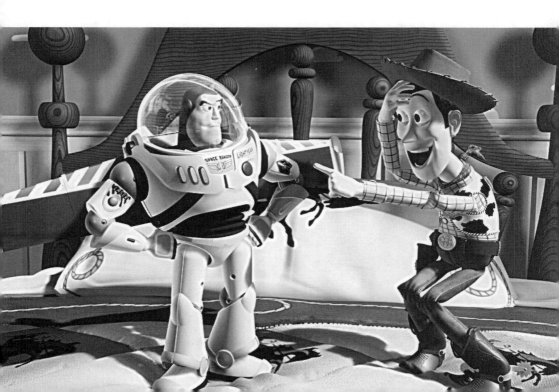

49. What is the name of the film that stars Sinbad as secret service agent Sam Simms who is assigned to protect Luke Davenport, the president's son?

50. In 1996, Disney released a live-action version of the full-length animated classic *One Hundred and One Dalmatians* (1961). Which actress played the despicable Cruella De Vil?

Walt Disney
Pictures

Answers

1. *Victory Through Air Power* (1943). The film was released only once.
2. *The Living Desert* (1953). The three previous live-action features were filmed in the United Kingdom.
3. The 1954 feature *20,000 Leagues Under the Sea.*
4. *Johnny Tremain* (1957).
5. Peter Ellenshaw.
6. *The Absent-Minded Professor* (1961).
7. *The Shaggy Dog* (1959), *The Absent-Minded Professor* (1961), and *Son of Flubber* (1963). In 1994 Touchstone released *Ed Wood*, which was filmed in black and white. In addition, many early cartoons and two recent short-subject films, *Frankenweenie* and *Vincent*, were also produced in black and white.
8. The characters Merlin and Arthur were in *Unidentified Flying Oddball* (1979) and *A Kid in King Arthur's Court* (1995).
9. The film is set in Scotland in the year 1912.
10. Actress Pola Negri played Madame Habib in *The Moon-Spinners* (1964).
11. The song "Stay Awake," which Mary Poppins sang to the children in an effort to put them to sleep.
12. Mary Poppins is willing to give George Banks a "one-week trial period" and she "needs every second Tuesday off."
13. "Step in Time."
14. Actress Jane Darwell came out of retirement to portray the old birdwoman. Darwell received an Academy Award for her work in the film *The Grapes of Wrath* (1940).
15. *Those Calloways* (1965).
16. Actor Tom Skerritt appeared in *Those Calloways.*
17. All three were considered for the role of Anthony J. Drexel Biddle in the 1967 film *The Happiest Millionaire.*
18. Written by Cordelia Drexel Biddle and Kyle Crichton, the book *My Philadelphia Father* relates the true-life story of the eccentric millionaire Anthony J. Drexel Biddle in the 1967 film *The Happiest Millionaire.*
19. The song "It Won't Be Long 'Til Christmas" was sung by MacMurray and Garson. Interestingly, the film was heavily edited before its initial release, with one of the casualties being the song. It wasn't until

seventeen years later that the sequence was added to the film for a Disney Channel showing.

20. *Bedknobs and Broomsticks* (1971). The song was edited from the film because Radio City Music Hall, the theater that debuted the film, had strict scheduling obligations.

21. *One Little Indian* (1973).

22. *Midnight Madness* (1980).

23. *Trenchcoat* (1983), which stars Margot Kidder.

24. Shakespeare's *Macbeth* provided the inspiration to author Ray Bradbury for his book and the film *Something Wicked This Way Comes* (1983).

25. The carnival's carousel.

26. The villain Beauty Smith is a character from the 1991 film *White Fang*.

27. The four represent members of the 1988 Jamaican Olympic bobsled team in the film *Cool Runnings* (1993).

28. Sanka Coffie, played by actor Doug E. Doug, used to place an egg under his helmet for good luck. Sanka would also give the egg a kiss before placing it under the helmet.

29. The coach, Irv, a former Olympian bobsledder, played by actor John Candy.

30. The song "All for Love" was featured in the 1993 film *The Three Musketeers*. The three popular vocalists who performed the song were Rod Stewart, Sting, and Bryan Adams.

31. The Canadian city of Winnipeg, Manitoba, provided the start for the 522-mile race, which finished in St. Paul, Minnesota.

32. Preston writes the check out for cash in the amount of one million dollars.

33. The Junior Goodwill Games.

34. The nasty team from Finland faces off against the Ducks in the finals.

35. The expression "hakuna matata" was used in the 1989 film *Cheetah*, and the song is heard in the 1995 film *Toy Story*.

36. Audiences were treated to the film *Angels in the Outfield* for its world premiere at Three Rivers Stadium in Pittsburgh, Pennsylvania. The city played host that year to Major League Baseball's 65th All-Star Game.

37. Whenever Roger sees an angel he flaps his arms in a flying motion.

38. *Squanto: A Warrior's Tale* (1994).

39. The business card reads: "If something should happen to me, put on my suit, the reindeer will know what to do." In fine print is the following: "Santa Clause: In putting on this suit and entering the sleigh, the wearer waives any and all rights to previous identity, real or implied, and fully accepts the duties and responsibilities of Santa Claus until such time

that wearer becomes unable to do so either by accident or design."

40. A magical snow globe.

41. Kitty (Katherine) presented Mowgli with a bracelet when the two were very young, and it is how the two were able to recognize each other when they were older.

42. *The Big Green* (1995).

43. The film *Frank and Ollie* details the life of Disney animators Frank Thomas and Ollie Johnston. The film was produced by Frank's son, Theodore Thomas, and follows the careers of these two animators through their work on *Snow White and the Seven Dwarfs* (1937) and many other Disney films.

44. Actress Ann Jillian portrayed Little Bo Peep in the film *Babes in Toyland* (1961) and actress Annie Potts supplied the voice of the character in *Toy Story* (1995).

45. Buzz Lightyear.

46. Actor-comedian Tim Allen provides the voice of Space Ranger Buzz Lightyear and Academy Award–winning actor Tom Hanks supplies the voice of Cowboy Woody.

47. James accidentally spills the contents of the bag onto the base of a peach tree, causing the fruit to grow to an enormous size. James later crawls into the giant peach and his journey begins.

48. Jack makes a cameo appearance in the 1996 feature *James and the Giant Peach*. In the movie's underwater sequence, the character Centipede attempts to steal a compass from a pirate ship and the skeletons come alive with Captain Jack leading them. Both of these films were stop-action movies made by the production company Skellington.

49. *First Kid* (1996).

50. Glenn Close portrayed the villain Cruella De Vil in the 1996 live-action remake.

Touchstone
Pictures

Questions

1. What name does the mermaid choose when she becomes human and comes on land in the 1984 film *Splash*?

2. At the conclusion of the film *Splash*, what becomes of the mermaid and Allen Bauer?

3. Academy Award–winning actress Jessica Lange stars in which 1984 film about a family named Ivy trying to save their Iowa farm from the threat of foreclosure?

4. Which film is about a scientist and his wife who, while studying rare fossils in the heart of the African rain forests, uncover a pair of brontosaurs and their hatchling dinosaur?

5. Which 1986 film stars legendary actors Kirk Douglas and Burt Lancaster as two old-fashioned train robbers released from prison only to realize that normal life proves a difficult transition?

6. This 1987 comedy stars Bette Midler and Shelley Long as two aspiring actresses who become rivals on stage as well as in real life when they both discover they are smitten by the same man.

7. Which 1987 film stars Danny DeVito and Richard Dreyfuss as two aluminum siding salesman who are constantly feuding?

8. Prior to providing the voice of the Genie in *Aladdin* (1992), which two characters were portrayed by Robin Williams in Touchstone films?

9. In the film *Big Business* (1988), which two actresses play the roles of two sets of twin sisters mixed up at birth who eventually discover that mistake later in life?

10. What musical group recorded the popular song "Kokomo" used in the film *Cocktail* (1988)?

11. Which 1988 film set in the 1970s is about the son of an avid

Elvis fan who kidnaps the King of Rock 'n' Roll one day when he is performing at a nearby concert?

12. Which two actresses play the part of CC Bloom, one as an eleven-year-old and the other as an adult in the 1989 film *Beaches*?

13. Which 1990 film had a working title of *Three Thousand*?

14. How many Academy Awards did the film *Dick Tracy* (1990) win?

15. Which Touchstone film was the first to have a sequel?

16. Which comedy film stars Bill Murray and Richard Dreyfuss as a patient and a doctor who strike up an unusual relationship?

17. What causes the authorities to arrest George Banks in the film *Father of the Bride* (1991)?

18. What gift does Bryan MacKenzie give to Annie Banks, which causes the temporary cancellation of their wedding in the film *Father of the Bride* (1991)?

19. After witnessing a mob-style shooting in the film *Sister Act* (1992), where do the authorities decide to hide Deloris and what new name is she given?

20. Which 1993 film received an Academy Award nomination for both Best Actress and Best Actor?

21. In the film *Tim Burton's The Nightmare Before Christmas* (1993), who does Jack Skellington aspire to be after falling through a door marked "Christmastown"?

22. Which popular late-night talk show host made a cameo appearance, which also happened to be his film debut, in the 1994 film *Cabin Boy*?

23. Which 1994 film tells the true-life story of an eccentric actor, writer, and director who was constantly trying to win the approval of his fellow Hollywood peers by releasing some of the more memorable horror films of all time?

24. What is the name of the comedy film starring actress Ellen DeGeneres in her eagerly anticipated major motion picture debut?

25. Which 1996 action thriller stars Mel Gibson as an airline mogul who will stop at nothing to see the return of his kidnapped son and the proper punishment of the criminals responsible?

Touchstone
Pictures

Answers

1. The mermaid chooses the name Madison after seeing it on a street sign in New York City.

2. Madison has no other choice but to return to the waters in an effort to escape from the authorities who are pursuing her when they discover she is a mermaid. Allen Bauer must choose to follow her to the waters or remain on land; he decides to follow Madison.

3. *Country*. Lange, in addition to starring in the role of Jewell Ivy, also served as a co-producer.

4. *Baby: Secret of the Lost Legend* (1985).

5. Douglas and Lancaster play two notorious ex-criminals Long and Doyle in *Tough Guys* (1986). After coming to the realization that life outside of prison is too much of a transition for them, the two set out again in a life of crime.

6. The 1987 comedy film is *Outrageous Fortune*. Unfortunately, Midler and Long, playing the parts of Sandy and Lauren, discover the man they are smitten by is actually a traitor ready to expose national secrets to the Russian KGB.

7. *Tin Men* (1987).

8. In *Good Morning, Vietnam* (1987), he starred as Adrian Cronauer, and in *Dead Poets Society* (1989), he played John Keating.

9. Actresses Lily Tomlin and Bette Midler.

10. The Beach Boys.

11. *Heartbreak Hotel* (1988).

12. Actress Mayim Bialik plays the role of CC Bloom as a young girl and Bette Midler plays her as an adult. Bialik received much praise after the part and soon landed a starring role in her own television series, *Blossom*, with Touchstone.

13. The 1990 film *Pretty Woman*, was originally going to be called *Three Thousand*, which was based on the amount Edward Lewis was willing to pay Vivian to be his date for the week.

14. The film *Dick Tracy* captured three Academy Awards including Best Makeup, Best Art Direction/Set Direction, and Best Original Song for "Sooner or Later."

15. *Three Men and a Baby* was released in 1987, followed in 1990 by *Three Men and a Little Lady*.

16. *What About Bob?* In the film, Bob, played by Murray, suffers from a collection of phobias, paranoia, and delusions. One of those delusions is that Bob thinks he has struck up a great friendship with Dr. Marvin, played by Dreyfuss. Dr. Marvin has no desire to be Bob's best buddy.

17. George was arrested for removing hot dog buns from a package because he refused to pay for twelve buns when there were only eight hot dogs in the pack.

18. A blender.

19. Deloris, played by actress Whoopi Goldberg, is placed in a convent in San Francisco called St. Francis, and she is given the name Sister Mary Clarence.

20. The 1993 film *What's Love Got to Do with It* earned an Academy Award nomination for Angela Bassett as Best Actress and the Best Actor nomination for Laurence Fishburne.

21. Jack wants to be the new Santa Claus, or as he puts it, "Sandy Claws." Jack accomplishes this after sending Lock, Shock, and Barrel to kidnap the real Santa Claus.

22. David Letterman.

23. *Ed Wood* (1994). Some of the films for which Wood was responsible have become cult classics.

24. *Mr. Wrong* (1996).

25. *Ransom* (1996).

Hollywood
Pictures

Questions

1. Name the film starring Rebecca DeMornay as a live-in nanny determined to destroy a family she blames for the death of her husband.

2. Which 1992 film set in the Amazon rain forest tells the story of an eccentric scientist, Dr. Robert Campbell, and his search for the cure for cancer?

3. Which film features the character Shirlee Kenyon, who accidentally lands a job as an on-air radio personality in Chicago and quickly becomes a favorite with listeners?

4. Which 1992 film features two high school oddballs, Dave and Stoney, who unearth a frozen prehistoric man in their very own backyard?

5. Which film set in Germany during the reign of Hitler tells the story of two youths and their love for American music, outlawed by the Nazi-controlled government?

6. Which film stars Patrick Swayze as Jack Charles, a small-town crook who must decide between the crime of his life or life with his children?

7. Which film, based on a best-selling book by Amy Tan, tells the story of a group of women who gather to reminisce during their weekly game of mah-jongg?

8. What city provides the setting for the film *Money for Nothing* (1993), and how much money did Joey Coyle recover?

9. Which well-known Disney actor played the role of the legendary lawman Wyatt Earp in the 1993 film *Tombstone*?

10. Which 1994 film stars Pauly Shore in the role of Bones Conway, who joins the Army to take advantage of its medical benefits, exclusive PX shopping, and a steady income?

11. What is the name of the real-life television quiz show that captivated millions during the 1950s and provided the basis for the film *Quiz Show* (1994)?

12. What is the name of the popular actor who was nominated for an Academy Award for Best Director for the film *Quiz Show*?

13. Which actress plays the role of Lucy, a Chicago Transit Authority worker, in the film *While You Were Sleeping* (1995)?

14. Which actress plays the role of Elsie, the grandmother, in *While You Were Sleeping*?

15. What is the name of the submarine featured in the 1995 action thriller *Crimson Tide*?

16. What is the name of the 1995 action adventure starring Sylvester Stallone as a futuristic judge genetically created to enforce the law?

17. What 1995 film is based on a true-life best-selling book by teacher LouAnne Johnson?

18. Which 1995 drama is based on a literary classic by Nathaniel Hawthorne?

19. What Academy Award–winning actor portrayed the part of Richard Nixon in the 1995 film that details the life of the thirty-seventh president?

20. What is the name of the 1995 film that stars Richard Dreyfuss as a music teacher who inspires the respect and dedication of his students?

21. Where did the film *The Rock* (1996) hold its world premiere?

22. Legendary actor Sean Connery has appeared in two Hollywood Pictures films, *Medicine Man* (1992) and *The Rock* (1996). Which two songs does Sean Connery sing in each of the films?

23. What popular actor stars in the 1996 film *Jack*, the story of a ten-year old boy named Jack Powell who suffers from a genetic condition that makes him appear four times older than his actual age?

24. In the film *Jack* (1996), which popular actor plays Lawrence Woodruff, Jack's private tutor?

25. Which actress-entertainer stars in the true-life story of Eva Perón and her dictator husband Juan Perón during his rise to power in Argentina during the 1940s?

Hollywood Pictures

Answers

1. *The Hand That Rocks the Cradle* (1992).
2. *Medicine Man* (1992), starring Sean Connery as Dr. Robert Campbell. Problems arise when Campbell loses the formula and a race against time ensues to recover the antidote.
3. *Straight Talk*, starring Dolly Parton as Shirlee Kenyon, the WNDY radio station personality.
4. *Encino Man* (1992) stars Brendan Fraser as the frozen prehistoric man who thaws and is disguised by Dave and Stoney as a visiting exchange student from Estonia.
5. *Swing Kids* (1993).
6. *Father Hood* (1993).
7. *The Joy Luck Club* (1993).
8. The true story of Joey Coyle, who recovered a bag of money dropped from an armored car, was set in Philadelphia. The amount was $1.2 million.
9. Actor Kurt Russell played the role of the legendary lawman Wyatt Earp. Russell has appeared in a total of eleven Disney feature films, several television shows, and also provided a voice for the 1981 full-length animated feature, *The Fox and the Hound*.
10. *In the Army Now* (1994).
11. *Twenty-One*. Millions of television viewers were captivated with the program, only to find out the show was rigged.
12. Robert Redford was the Academy Award nominee for Best Director.
13. Sandra Bullock.
14. Elsie was portrayed by actress Glynis Johns. Johns began her Disney career in 1953 with the film *The Sword and the Rose*. The popular British actress also played Mrs. Banks in *Mary Poppins* (1964).
15. USS *Alabama*. The action thriller stars Gene Hackman and Denzel Washington as two military officials faced with the ultimate decision of nuclear disaster.
16. Sylvester Stallone stars in *Judge Dredd* (1995) as a futuristic law enforcement agent who has been genetically designed to act in the capacity of judge, jury, and executioner. The character was first developed in comic books.

17. *Dangerous Minds* (1995). The film was based on the book *My Posse Don't Do Homework.* The film, starring Michelle Pfeiffer, details the true-life experiences of LouAnne Johnson and her attempts to teach English to a class of tough inner-city teenagers. A television series by the same name, starring Annie Potts, debuted in 1996 due to the success of the film.

18. *The Scarlet Letter*, which stars actress Demi Moore.

19. Actor Anthony Hopkins stars in the film *Nixon.* The film itself captured four Academy Award nominations.

20. *Mr. Holland's Opus.* Dreyfuss received an Academy Award nomination for his portrayal in the film.

21. The film *The Rock* appropriately held its world premiere at Alcatraz federal penitentiary, which also provided the setting for the action thriller. Alcatraz was considered to be America's most inescapable prison from 1934 to 1963. The film stars Academy Award winners Sean Connery and Nicolas Cage as unlikely partners who must save San Francisco from a poison gas threat from a renegade military officer.

22. In the film *Medicine Man*, Connery sings "That Old Black Magic," and in *The Rock* he sings "San Francisco." Connery has appeared in only one other Disney film. *Darby O'Gill and the Little People* (1959), in which he performed the song, "Pretty Irish Girl."

23. Robin Williams plays Jack.

24. Bill Cosby.

25. Madonna portrays Eva Perón in the 1996 film *Evita.*

Walt Disney Theatrical Productions

....

Questions

1. In which New York theater did *Disney's Beauty and the Beast* make its Broadway debut?

2. Which actor is the only individual to receive credit in both the 1991 full-length animated feature and the theatrical production of *Disney's Beauty and the Beast*?

3. How many Tony Award nominations did *Disney's Beauty and the Beast* receive after its first year on Broadway?

4. Which song was originally scheduled to debut in the 1991 animated version but was dropped from the film and eventually found its way into the theatrical production?

5. What popular French actor provided the inspiration for the character Lumiere?

6. What popular television actor portrayed the character Maurice when *Disney's Beauty and the Beast* made its debut on Broadway?

7. How many new songs were developed for *Disney's Beauty and the Beast* when the story was introduced to theater audiences?

8. What love song does the Beast sing at the conclusion of Act I?

9. Due to the success of *Disney's Beauty and the Beast* on Broadway, six touring companies were added. In which cities did they debut?

10. What is the name of the famous theater on 42nd Street in New York City that was purchased by The Walt Disney Company in 1994?

Walt Disney Theatrical Productions

Answers

1. The Palace Theater served as the home for the Broadway production of *Disney*'s *Beauty and the Beast* when it premiered on April 18, 1994.

2. Actor David Ogden Stiers provided the narration in the 1991 full-length animated feature as well as the theatrical production of *Disney*'s *Beauty and the Beast*. Stiers also provided the voice of the character Cogsworth in the animated version.

3. *Disney*'s *Beauty and the Beast* received a total of nine nominations at the 48th Annual Tony Awards. The production captured one Tony Award for the category of Best Costume Design by Ann Hould-Ward. According to reports, Ann Hould-Ward developed some 350 sketches for the production. The other nominations were Best Musical Score, Best Book, Best Director, Best Actor, Best Actress, Best Featured Actor, Best Lighting Design, and Best Musical.

4. The song "Human Again" was cut from the 1991 full-length animated feature but was then added to the theatrical production.

5. The character Lumiere was inspired by French actor Maurice Chevalier.

6. Actor Tom Bosley portrayed Belle's father Maurice. Bosley may be best remembered in his role of Mr. Cunningham on the long-running television series *Happy Days*.

7. A total of six new songs were written for the theatrical production. The team of Alan Menken and Howard Ashman provided the original score for the 1991 feature. After the untimely death of Howard Ashman, lyricist Tim Rice joined Menken to develop the additional songs.

8. "If I Can't Love Her."

9. The six cities included Los Angeles, Minneapolis, Toronto, Tokyo, Vienna, and Melbourne, Australia.

10. The Walt Disney Company purchased the New Amsterdam Theatre in 1994. Constructed in 1903, it was nicknamed "the House Beautiful" and served as home for the famous Ziegfeld Follies. After three years of restoration, it opened in 1997, with its first Disney production being the concert event *King David*, developed by the creative talents of Alan Menken and Tim Rice.

Disney Sports Enterprises

Questions

1. What is the name of the Anaheim arena where the Mighty Ducks play their regular season games?

2. What is the name of the Mighty Ducks' official mascot?

3. Who are the Duck Decoys?

4. Against which team did the Mighty Ducks capture their first regular season victory?

5. In 1994, the Mighty Ducks teamed up with the Pittsburgh Penguins to purchase a financial interest in which former Communist hockey team?

6. In which year did the first Walt Disney World Marathon take place?

7. The Walt Disney Company teamed up with the Indy Racing League to bring world-class racing events to the Walt Disney World Resort. When was the inaugural race of the Indy 200 at Walt Disney World?

8. In 1996, The Walt Disney Company purchased a 25 percent interest in which Major League baseball team?

9. What is the name of the sports complex located at the Walt Disney World Resort?

10. Which Major League baseball team signed an agreement to play their next twenty years of spring training baseball at the Walt Disney World Resort beginning in 1998?

Disney Sports Enterprises

Answers

1. The Mighty Ducks play their regular season home games at Arrowhead Pond. In 1995, a separate site was built to serve as the practice facility for the Mighty Ducks known as Disney ICE. Disney ICE, located in downtown Anaheim, serves the needs of the National Hockey League team as well as the community.
2. Wild Wing.
3. The Duck Decoys are the Mighty Ducks' cheerleading squad.
4. The Mighty Ducks captured their first regular season victory on October 13, 1993, against the Edmonton Oilers, defeating them with a score of 4 to 3 on home ice.
5. The two teams purchased a financial interest in the powerful Soviet Red Army Team. The Soviet Red Army Team successfully captured many world titles as well as several Olympic gold medals.
6. The first Walt Disney World Marathon took place in 1994.
7. The first race was held on January 27, 1996, and Buzz Calkins captured the inaugural title.
8. In 1996, The Walt Disney Company purchased a 25 percent interest in the California Angels from their owner, Gene Autry.
9. The facility is known as Disney's Wide World of Sports. The 200-acre complex offers state-of-the-art facilities to accommodate sporting events ranging from archery to weight lifting. Disney's Wide World of Sports complex is also the home of the Harlem Globetrotters, serving as the basketball team's training camp, and of the Amateur Athletic Union (AAU).
10. The Atlanta Braves.

Disneyland

Main Street, USA

Questions

1. Which railroad company was originally involved in the sponsorship of the Disneyland Railroad?

2. What was the original name of the Plaza Inn at Disneyland?

3. Which company originally sponsored the Main Street Pharmacy?

4. When the Disneyana Shop moved to its present location on the east side of Main Street, what kind of shop did it displace?

5. Featured on the second-story windows of Main Street, USA, are a collection of names honoring those individuals who have contributed to the success of Disneyland. Above which shop can you find the name of Walt Disney's father?

6. Who was the first human to be re-created in *Audio-Animatronics* form?

7. In what year did the Main Street Electrical Parade make its debut?

8. What was the name of the Main Street, USA, restaurant sponsored by the American Egg Board?

9. Where is the Fifth Freedom Mural?

10. What was the theme song of the Main Street Electrical Parade?

Main Street, USA

Answers

1. Santa Fe.
2. The Red Wagon Inn. The Main Street, USA restaurant was sponsored by Swift and was named after its logo, a red wagon.
3. The Upjohn Company served as the sponsor for the Main Street Pharmacy from 1955 to 1970. The shop then became the New Century Clock Shop.
4. A jewelry shop.
5. The name Elias Disney can be found above the Emporium. The window reads, "Elias Disney, Contractor."
6. Abraham Lincoln was the first human *Audio-Animatronics* figure to be developed. The figure is featured in the attraction Great Moments with Mr. Lincoln.
7. The popular Main Street Electrical Parade made its debut on June 17, 1972, and took its last run in 1996.
8. The name of the restaurant was the American Egg House, which opened in 1978 and served guests up to the year 1983. The facility later became the Town Square Cafe.
9. Located at the exit from Great Moments with Mr. Lincoln, the artwork is a fifty-three-foot mural that pays special tribute to those individuals who achieved greatness as a result of the "Fifth Freedom"—that of free enterprise. Walt Disney himself is honored on the mural.
10. The synthesized sounds of "Baroque Hoedown" were heard as the theme song for the Main Street Electrical Parade.

Fantasyland

Questions

1. Why is Sleeping Beauty Castle significantly smaller than any other Magic Kingdom castle?

2. What is the primary building material that was used in the construction of Sleeping Beauty Castle?

3. Walt Disney originally referred to Sleeping Beauty Castle by what other name?

4. Which current attraction was originally planned as Disneyland's first roller coaster ride?

5. Which early proposed Fantasyland attraction was planned as a boat ride that would take guests through a mountain of candy?

6. What was the name of the attraction that preceded Storybook Land?

7. Which two Fantasyland attractions were inspired by the 1941 full-length animated feature *Dumbo*?

8. How many horses can be found on King Arthur Carrousel?

9. Which company used to sponsor the Pirate Ship and Restaurant anchored in Skull Rock Cove?

10. The "patchwork quilt" featured in Storybook Land was inspired by which 1933 animated short?

11. Which Disneyland attraction opened in 1956 and remained in operation until 1994?

12. What attraction can be found inside Sleeping Beauty Castle?

13. What was the first roller coaster to run more than one car per track simultaneously?

14. In which attraction will a guest find the phrase "Verdict First, Sentence Afterward"?

15. Besides opening day for Disneyland on July 17, 1955, what was the only other day that the Sleeping Beauty Castle drawbridge was officially lowered?

16. Which character is featured on the front of each and every ride vehicle in Pinocchio's Daring Journey?

17. An image of what character magically turns into a cloud of sparkles in Pinocchio's Daring Journey?

18. Which attraction has been referred to as "The Happiest Cruise that Ever Sailed the Seven Seas"?

19. Which character's footprints are found along the pathway outside Alice in Wonderland?

20. The ride vehicles for Alice in Wonderland are in the shape of which character?

Fantasyland

Answers

1. During the development of Sleeping Beauty Castle, Walt Disney recalled the many stories concerning the building of the European castles. Often, the huge and imposing castles were built in order to intimidate the poor peasants. Walt Disney believed a smaller castle would represent a friendly castle.

2. Although it may appear to be constructed mostly of stone, the primary building material is actually wood.

3. During a television show, Walt Disney originally referred to the castle as Snow White's Castle. The full-length animated feature *Sleeping Beauty*, which served as the inspiration for the name of the castle, would not debut in theaters until 1959, four years after the opening of Disneyland.

4. Casey Jr. Circus Train.

5. The name of the proposed attraction was Big Rock Candy Mountain. At the end of the attraction, guests would enter an area featuring characters from *The Wizard of Oz* (1939).

6. When Disneyland opened, the unfinished attraction that would later become Storybook Land was known as Canal Boats of the World.

7. Casey Jr. Circus Train and Dumbo the Flying Elephant.

8. Guests have a choice of seventy-two horses on King Arthur Carrousel.

9. Chicken of the Sea tuna was the sponsor for the fast-food facility from 1955 through 1969.

10. *Lullaby Land.*

11. The Skyway officially opened on June 23, 1956, and closed on November 9, 1994. The attraction was dedicated by Walt Disney and the Swiss consul general of Los Angeles, Dr. Walter Schmid. It was also the first tramway of its kind to operate in the United States. To commemorate the closing of the attraction. Mickey and Minnie took the last "official" ride on the Skyway.

12. In 1957, Walt Disney, in an effort to utilize the unused space inside Sleeping Beauty Castle, opened a walk-through attraction featuring dioramas retelling the story of *Sleeping Beauty* (1959).

13. The Matterhorn Bobsleds, which opened in 1959.

14. Alice in Wonderland.

15. The drawbridge was lowered on May 25, 1983, when a completely new

and redesigned Fantasyland opened in Disneyland. The redesigned Fantasyland featured a collection of new facades themed to the various animated films, as well as the addition of a completely new attraction, Pinocchio's Daring Journey.

16. Jiminy Cricket.
17. An image of the Blue Fairy magically disappears at the end of the attraction.
18. It's a Small World.
19. The White Rabbit's.
20. The Caterpillar.

Tomorrowland

Questions

1. What was the title of the first film to be shown at Disneyland in 1955 utilizing the Circle-Vision 360 photography process?

2. TWA and McDonnell-Douglas, each at different times, sponsored which early Disneyland attraction?

3. What name was given to the timepiece that depicted the different time zones from around the world during the early days of Disneyland?

4. What was the name of the Tomorrowland gift shop that opened in 1956 and sold animation cels for $1.25 to $3.00 apiece?

5. Where could guests find actual "mermaids" in Tomorrowland?

6.   What attraction did the United States Navy at one point express interest in sponsoring?

7.   What was the original color of the submarines in Submarine Voyage at Disneyland?

8.   What famous German rocket scientist helped in the development of the Disneyland attraction Flight to the Moon?

9.   What has been considered the predecessor of the Disneyland monorail system?

10. What company helped produce the original monorail system?

11. What is the name of the Tomorrowland attraction that enabled guests to float in vehicles on a cushion of air utilizing a concept similar to hovercraft boats?

12. What attraction included a trip into a molecule?

13. What company sponsored the structure known as the House of the Future?

14. What was the name of the *Audio-Animatronics* individual who served as the operations director at the Mission Control Center for the Flight to the Moon attraction?

15. Which character served as the narrator for the attraction America Sings?

Tomorrowland

Answers

1. Circle-Vision 360 was originally referred to as Circarama, and the original film was *Circarama U.S.A. (A Tour of the West)*, sponsored by American Motors.

2. The attraction was known as Rocket to the Moon. It later became Flight to the Moon and Mission to Mars.

3. The timepiece was called the Clock of the World and it marked the entrance to Tomorrowland.

4. The Art Corner.

5. Several times in Disneyland's history, live "mermaids" could be found on the rocks in the Submarine Voyage lagoon.

6. The Submarine Voyage, but it was decided that the General Dynamics Corporation would do the honors.

7. The original eight submarines were painted gray to resemble the first group of U.S. nuclear submarines, which were commissioned in the late 1950s. Today, they are bright yellow to resemble scientific research vessels.

8. Wernher von Braun.

9. The Viewliner, which operated from 1957 to 1958, was considered the predecessor of the Disneyland monorail. Walt Disney referred to the Viewliner as the "Train of Tomorrow."

10. The Swiss company that helped produce the original Monorail system was also part of its original name, the Disneyland-Alweg Monorail System.

11. The Flying Saucers used this technology from 1961 to 1966.

12. Adventure Thru Inner Space.

13. From 1957 until 1967 the House of the Future was sponsored by Monsanto. The house itself was made of synthetic materials and featured the latest in appliances and furniture as it attempted to reveal what life would be like in the future.

14. Mr. Tom Morrow, a play on the word Tomorrow, was the Operations Director.

15. Sam the Eagle, voiced by Burl Ives.

Adventureland

Questions

1. Who are Collette, Susette, Mimi, Fifi, Gigi, and Josephine in the Enchanted Tiki Room?

2. What is considered the National Anthem for the Enchanted Tiki Room attraction?

3. In which attraction can you hear the songs "Swisskapolka" and "Animal Carnival?"

4. What is *Disneyodendron semperflorens grandis*?

5. What popular filmmaker did The Walt Disney Company team up with in order to create the Indiana Jones Adventure?

6. What is the name of the mysterious temple deity featured in the Indiana Jones Adventure?

7. What are the names of the three inner halls that determine the fate of each guest after they leave the great Chamber of Destiny in the Indiana Jones Adventure?

8. What movie prop found outside the Indiana Jones Adventure was originally used in the feature film *Raiders of the Lost Ark* (1981)?

9. Which actor from the *Indiana Jones* films can be heard over the radio receiver as one rides in troop transport vehicles through the Indiana Jones Adventure?

10. Which two attractions were shifted and modified in order to build the Indiana Jones Adventure?

Adventureland

Answers

1. The six white cockatoos make up the Ladies of the Chorus in the Enchanted Tiki Room.
2. "Let's All Sing Like the Birdies Sing."
3. Swiss Family Tree House.
4. When translated, the words mean "large ever-blooming Disney tree." The phrase is used to represent the fabricated tree constructed for the Swiss Family Tree House attraction.
5. George Lucas. Lucas also collaborated in two other Disneyland attractions, Captain Eo and Star Tours.
6. Mara.
7. The three halls are Chamber of Earthly Riches, Fountain of Eternal Youth, and the Observatory of the Future.
8. The prop that is on display outside the attraction is the actual German patrol truck that was used in the classic scene pitting Indy against a platoon of soldiers while aboard the vehicle.
9. The character Sallah from the *Indiana Jones* films, portrayed by actor John Rhys-Davies, can be heard over the radio receiver.
10. The Monorail and the Jungle Cruise.

Frontierland
and Critter Country

Questions

1. During the early days of Disneyland, what was the name of the Sheriff of Frontierland?

2. What company originally sponsored the Golden Horseshoe Saloon?

3. What was the name of the original Frontierland Pancake House?

4. Why is there a petrified tree located on the banks of the Rivers of America?

5. The term *Audio-Animatronics* was used first in association with which attraction?

6. Where did the construction of the *Mark Twain* Steamboat superstructure take place?

7. Which attraction features a combination of songs that include "Come Back Sweet Papa," "Milanbury Joys," and "Western Saloon"?

8. Tom Sawyer Island was officially annexed and recognized by the legislature from which state?

9. Which Frontierland attraction opened in 1979 and was later included in each of the other three Magic Kingdom theme parks?

10. What is the name of the small town featured in the Big Thunder Mountain Railroad attraction?

11. Which year appears over the entrance to the building that houses the Golden Horseshoe?

12. The Sailing Ship *Columbia* at Disneyland becomes what character's ship during the nighttime spectacular, Fantasmic!?

13. Prior to being called Critter Country, what was this themed land's original name?

14. Davy Crockett's Explorer Canoes were originally referred to by what other name?

15. Prior to being referred to as the Brer Bar, what was the name of this Critter Country refreshment facility?

Frontierland
and Critter Country

Answers

1. Sheriff Lucky. One of his major tasks was keeping the cardsharp, Black Bart, in line.
2. The show was originally known as the Golden Horseshoe Revue and its first sponsor was Pepsi-Cola (from 1955 to 1982).
3. The Aunt Jemima Pancake House was the name of the original Frontierland restaurant. It is currently known as the River Belle Terrace.
4. The petrified tree was a gift given by Walt Disney to his wife, Lillian, for their thirty-first wedding anniversary in 1956. The tree is from the Pike Petrified Forest in Colorado.
5. The term was used first in association with the Nature's Wonderland attraction in 1960. The attraction's figures were, however, not as sophisticated as what would later be known as *Audio-Animatronics*.
6. The construction of the superstructure of the *Mark Twain* Steamboat took place at the Walt Disney Studios in Burbank, California. The hull was constructed at the Todd Shipyards in San Pedro, California.
7. They are some of the songs that guests can hear during a ride on the *Mark Twain* Steamboat. The song "Milanbury Joys" was actually performed by the Firehouse Five Plus Two, a musical group created by Walt Disney Studio employees.
8. Missouri.
9. Big Thunder Mountain Railroad.
10. The current name of the small town is Big Thunder and it is a re-creation of a traditional mining town. The town's original name was Rainbow Ridge. At the Walt Disney World version of the attraction the small town is known as Tumbleweed.
11. 1871. The building itself has served as the home for thousands of daily performances. Walt Disney himself used to enjoy occasional performances from his favorite box located next to the stage.
12. The Sailing Ship *Columbia* becomes Captain Hook's ship during the nighttime spectacular, Fantasmic!
13. Its original name was Bear Country, beginning in 1972; the name was changed to Critter Country in 1988 with the addition of Splash Mountain.
14. They were known as the Indian War Canoes when they opened in 1956.
15. The Mile Long Bar.

New Orleans Square

Questions

1. While in Disneyland, where can one find Laffite's Landing?

2. Who wrote the theme song for Pirates of the Caribbean?

3. What is the name of the large pirate ship featured in Pirates of the Caribbean?

4. Which Disneyland attraction had its building completed six years before the attraction itself opened?

5. The actress who provided the voice of Maleficent from the full-length animated feature *Sleeping Beauty* (1959) also provides the voice for which character in the Haunted Mansion?

6. What does the weather vane perched atop the Haunted Mansion represent?

7. The names that are featured on the tombstones located outside of the Haunted Mansion refer to whom?

8. The organ located in the ballroom of the Haunted Mansion is a prop from which 1954 Disney film?

9. Which New Orleans Square attraction was the first to use and incorporate live actors and *Audio-Animatronics* together in an attraction?

10. What is the name of the private membership club located on the second floor in New Orleans Square?

New Orleans Square

Answers

1.   It is the dock where guests board the boats in Pirates of the Caribbean.
2.   The song "Yo Ho, Yo Ho, A Pirate's Life for Me" was written by one of the attraction's master designers, X. Atencio. Atencio also co-wrote the song heard in the Haunted Mansion, "Grim Grinning Ghosts."
3.   *Wicked Wench.*
4.   The Haunted Mansion.
5.   Actress Eleanor Audley, the voice of the evil Maleficent, also provides the voice of the mysterious head that appears inside the crystal ball in the Haunted Mansion. The character in the crystal ball is called Madame Leota. The live-action model for the figure was Lee Thomas, an artist and model designer for Walt Disney Imagineering.
6.   A clipper ship.
7.   The names that are featured on the tombstones are actually those of some of the attraction's original designers and developers, known as Imagineers. For example, one tombstone reads, "Master Gracey, laid to rest, No mourning please at his request." The name Master Gracey refers to Yale Gracey, one of the attraction's chief designers.
8.   It is the same organ that was played by Captain Nemo on his submarine in the 1954 film *20,000 Leagues Under the Sea.*
9.   The Haunted Mansion used live actors for a very short period of time. A live actor dressed in a suit of armor frightened anxious guests in the mansion's corridors.
10.   Club 33 is the name of Disneyland's prestigious private membership club created as a place where Disneyland corporate participants could entertain their guests. The number 33 simply refers to the street address. A similar club, which opened in 1983, can be found in Tokyo Disneyland.

Mickey's Toontown

Questions

1. What is Mickey's address in Mickey's Toontown?

2. What is the name of the location where guests can personally meet and visit with Mickey while in Mickey's Toontown?

3. What license plate number appears on Mickey's car in Mickey's Toontown?

4. Which character's house in Mickey's Toontown consists of inflatables, which allow guests to bounce off the walls, floors, furniture, and even the fireplace?

5. What is the name of the attraction that reflects the character Gadget's ever-resourceful and unique personality in a miniature roller coaster?

6. Instead of Benny the Cab from the feature film *Who Framed Roger Rabbit* (1988), what similar character can be found in Mickey's Toontown?

7. What is the name of the construction company found in Mickey's Toontown?

8. Which characters run the gas station and the diner in Mickey's Toontown?

9. What is the motto for Mickey's Toontown Hysterical Society?

10. The Toontown Train Depot was originally referred to by what two previous names?

Mickey's Toontown

Answers

1. According to some letters that appear on a table in Mickey's house, the address is: Mickey Mouse, 1 Neighborhood Lane, Mickey's Toontown.
2. Mickey meets and greets each of his fans at Mickey's Movie Barn Sound Stage.
3. MICKEY 1.
4. The shaky-looking structure is known as Goofy's Bounce House.
5. Gadget's Go-Coaster. The attraction takes guests on a fun-filled journey past a collection of oversized toys, combs, toothbrushes, and scissors, while riding in vehicles the shape of acorns.
6. The character Lenny the Cab joins Roger in Roger Rabbit's Car Toon Spin.
7. The Chinny Chin Chin Construction Company.
8. Goofy runs the gas station, which features fish in the gas tanks, and Daisy operates the diner.
9. "Laughter Is Sunshine You Can Hear."
10. The Videopolis Train Station and the Fantasyland Train Station.

Disneyland
Potpourri

Questions

1. What is the official street address of Disneyland?

2. The original Disneyland cast members' name tags were made of what two materials?

3. When were the "A," "B," "C," "D," and "E" attraction tickets first introduced to Disneyland guests?

4. Which official, representing the Soviet Union, was denied a trip to Disneyland by the U.S. State Department due to security issues?

5. What short-lived Disneyland area opened in 1957 outside the park's perimeter and was used for corporate picnics and special events?

6. What was the first themed land to be added to Disneyland after its opening in 1955?

7. Which astronaut affectionately referred to the excitement of her ride into space as a "real E ticket ride"?

8. Name the four "mountains" at Disneyland.

9. Including Main Street, USA, how many different stops does the Disneyland Railroad make as it circles the park?

10. A life-sized bronze statue of Walt Disney holding hands with Mickey Mouse can be found in what location at Disneyland park?

Disneyland Potpourri

Answers

1. The official street address of Disneyland is 1313 Harbor Boulevard.

2. For the first seven years of Disneyland, the cast members' name tags were made of brass and copper, then the switch was made to plastic name tags.

3. In October of 1955 the alpha tickets were introduced. The first were the "A," "B," and "C" tickets. In 1956 the "D" ticket was added and finally in 1959 the "E" ticket made its debut.

4. In 1959 Nikita Khrushchev was denied a visit, much to the disappointment of Walt Disney, who was eager to show his Disneyland park to the Soviet chairman.

5. The area was known as Holidayland and it was used for picnics and other special events from 1957 until 1961.

6. On July 24, 1966, New Orleans Square became the first new themed land to debut after the official grand opening of Disneyland in 1955.

7. America's first woman in space, Astronaut Sally Ride.

8. The four mountains are Splash Mountain; Big Thunder Mountain, home of Big Thunder Mountain Railroad; the Matterhorn, home of the Matterhorn Bobsleds; and Space Mountain.

9. The Disneyland Railroad makes a total of four stops, including Main Street, USA; New Orleans Square; Mickey's Toontown; and Tomorrowland.

10. The statue can be found at the hub of Disneyland, at the end of Main Street, USA, in front of Sleeping Beauty Castle. The statue's designer is Blaine Gibson, a longtime artist and sculptor for The Walt Disney Company.

Walt Disney World Magic Kingdom

Main Street, USA

Questions

1. Elements of which Magic Kingdom attraction were discovered in the Yucatan?

2. In which direction do the trains of the Walt Disney World Railroad travel—clockwise or counterclockwise?

3. Which Disney full-length animated feature provided the inspiration and theming for Tony's Town Square Restaurant?

4. The first Disneyana shop at Walt Disney World was located in which Magic Kingdom themed land?

5. Name the short film shown at the Main Street Cinema, which details Mickey's first experience in Hollywood.

6. What is the name of the barbershop quartet that performs on Main Street, USA?

7. Which oil company once sponsored a Main Street, USA, attraction?

8. Name the first corporate sponsors of the following Main Street, USA shops: the New Century Clock Shop, the Card Shop, the Camera Center, and the Town Square Cafe.

9. What type of watercraft was previously seen in the waterways in front of Cinderella Castle?

10. As guests walk up Main Street, USA, what is the first themed land on the left-hand side?

Main Street, USA

Answers

1. The four locomotives that make up the Walt Disney World Railroad were all discovered in the Yucatan, where they had been used to haul freight. Disney personnel discovered the classic locomotives, purchased them, shipped them to Tampa, Florida, to be refurbished, and then transported them to Walt Disney World.

2. The Walt Disney World Railroad trains travel clockwise around the Magic Kingdom. For a short period of time, the trains did travel counterclockwise (and backward partway), during the construction of Splash Mountain.

3. *Lady and the Tramp* (1955) provided the inspiration for Tony's Town Square Restaurant. The character Tony is the likable Italian restaurant owner who serenades Tramp and Lady that one "bella notte."

4. The first Disneyana shop was located in Fantasyland.

5. The short film is known as *Mickey's Big Break* and it stars Roy E. Disney, Mel Brooks, Ed Begley, Jr., and Mickey Mouse.

6. The barbershop quartet is known as the Dapper Dans, and they perform daily outside of the Harmony Barber Shop. In Disneyland Paris a similar quartet entertains guests, but it is referred to as The Main Street Quartet.

7. The Gulf Oil Company sponsored the Walt Disney Story from 1973 to 1983.

8. Elgin-Helbros/Bradley sponsored the New Century Clock Shop, Hallmark the Card Shop, GAF the Camera Center, and Oscar Mayer the Town Square Cafe.

9. The Plaza Swan Boats could be found in the waterways in front of Cinderella Castle from 1973 until 1983.

10. Adventureland.

Fantasyland

Questions

1. When the Magic Kingdom was in the development and design stages, an apartment for the Disney family was planned in which structure?

2. In your best estimate, how many granite stone blocks did it take to construct Cinderella Castle?

3. How many dolls are featured in It's a Small World?

4. What is the oldest attraction located in Fantasyland?

5. Which was the first attraction to incorporate *Audio-Animatronics* figures of Disney animated characters?

6. Which character appears in the preshow for The Legend of the Lion King?

7. Which attraction's theme song opens with the words "It's a world of laughter, a world of tears; it's a world of hopes and a world of fears"?

8. In what shape are the ride vehicles in Snow White's Adventures?

9. Which character is positioned on top of the Dumbo the Flying Elephant attraction?

10. To help commemorate the twenty-fifth anniversary of the Walt Disney World Resort, what was Cinderella Castle transformed into?

Fantasyland

Answers

1. The Disney family apartment was originally planned in one of the upper levels of Cinderella Castle.

2. The answer is zero. Cinderella Castle is an architectural wonder; six hundred tons of steel were used for the framework, and fiberglass was used for the exterior and interior walls, sculpted to resemble granite.

3. A total of 234 dolls are in It's a Small World. Actually, there are a total of 553 *Audio-Animatronics* figures, ranging from children to animals.

4. Cinderella's Golden Carrousel was originally built in 1917 by the Philadelphia Toboggan Company for use at the Detroit Palace Garden Park. The carrousel later was moved to the Maplewood Olympic Park in New Jersey. When it arrived at the Magic Kingdom it went through a complete renovation and scenes from the full-length animated feature *Cinderella* (1950) were painted in the panels above the horses.

5. The Mickey Mouse Revue, which opened in 1971, was the first to incorporate *Audio-Animatronics* figures of Disney animated characters. The attraction was eventually moved to Tokyo Disneyland for its grand opening.

6. The mystic baboon Rafiki greets guests as he tells the story of Simba during the preshow for The Legend of the Lion King.

7. It's a Small World.

8. The ride vehicles in Snow White's Adventures are shaped like mine cars. Each mine car features the name of a Dwarf.

9. Dumbo's mouse friend Timothy, holding the "magic feather" that Dumbo originally believed helped him fly.

10. The Castle was transformed into a Cinderella Castle Cake, painted pink and decorated with a combination of candy, candles, and sprinkles.

Tomorrowland

Questions

1. Which Tomorrowland attraction was in a development and test stage for ten years before it opened?

2. What was the first attraction to operate on a system known as linear induction motors?

3. Which attraction was formerly referred to as Star Jets?

4. What is the name of the Circle-Vision 360 film shown at the attraction known as The Timekeeper?

5. Which popular actor supplies the voice for the *Audio-Animatronics* figure The Timekeeper in the Circle-Vision 360 film and attraction of that same name? Who is the voice of 9-Eye?

6. Which Tomorrowland attraction was the first thrill attraction to be operated by a computer?

7. What is the name of the organization that occupies The Tomorrowland Interplanetary Convention Center, home of The ExtraTERRORestrial Alien Encounter?

8. What is the name of the playful alien in The ExtraTERRORestrial Alien Encounter?

9. Name the four holidays featured in Walt Disney's Carousel of Progress.

10. What is the name of the lounge singer featured in Cosmic Ray's Starlight Cafe?

Tomorrowland

Answers

1. Space Mountain was in a development and test stage for ten years before its 1975 opening.
2. The WEDway PeopleMover was the first to operate on the linear induction motor technology, which involves a system that requires no moving parts. The WEDway PeopleMover became the Tomorrowland Transit Authority.
3. In 1994, Star Jets officially became Astro Orbiter.
4. The Circle-Vision 360 film is known as *From Time to Time*. The film was originally produced for Visionarium at Disneyland Paris. When the film was included at the Walt Disney World Magic Kingdom, English language dialogue and some American footage were added.
5. Robin Williams supplies the voice of The Timekeeper and actress Rhea Perlman is the voice of the character 9-Eye.
6. Space Mountain was the first thrill attraction to be operated by a computer. Space Mountain was also the first roller coaster of its kind to operate in perpetual darkness.
7. X-S Tech is the name of the organization led by the sinister Chairman Clench.
8. Skippy.
9. The four holidays are Valentine's Day, the Fourth of July, Halloween, and Christmas.
10. The lounge singer is known as Sonny Eclipse. Sonny also has a group of background singers known as the Space Angels.

Adventureland

Questions

1. What is the name of the 100-year-old alligator featured in the Jungle Cruise?

2. What is the name of the building that houses the Enchanted Tiki Birds in the attraction The Tropical Serenade?

3. The sign that appears at Swiss Family Tree House indicates the name of what ship?

4. What is the name of the *Audio-Animatronics* parrot featured at the entrance to Pirates of the Caribbean?

5. Which Adventureland attraction is set to debut a new show featuring the personalities of Iago and Zazu in 1998?

Adventureland

Answers

1. The 100-year-old alligator in the Jungle Cruise is affectionately referred to as Old Smiley.
2. The Sunshine Pavilion.
3. According to an inscription the name of the ship is the *Swallow*.
4. The parrot's name is Barker Bird.
5. The attraction currently known as The Tropical Serenade.

Frontierland

Questions

1. Where can guests find names such as I.M. Brave, U.B. Bold, and U.R. Courageous?

2. Which Frontierland attraction had originally been designed as a show for Walt Disney's planned Mineral King valley ski resort?

3. Who is considered the founder of Grizzly Hall, the playhouse and home of the Country Bear Jamboree?

4. What is the name of the large lumbering piano player at the Country Bear Jamboree?

5. Which bear sings the classic ballad "Blood on the Saddle" at the Country Bear Jamboree?

6. How many bears entertain guests at the Country Bear Jamboree?

7. What are the names of the three animal mounts featured on the wall at the Country Bear Jamboree?

8. In what year did Tom Sawyer Island open at Walt Disney World Magic Kingdom?

9. The Frontierland Railroad Station at the Walt Disney World Magic Kingdom was relocated at the time of construction of what other attraction?

10. What is the name of the small bear that sits on the side of the stage when the musical group the Five Bear Rugs perform?

Frontierland

Answers

1. They are some of the names that appear on the runaway trains for Big Thunder Mountain Railroad.
2. The Country Bear Jamboree.
3. Located above the main stage area is a picture of Grizzly Hall's founder, Ursus R. Bear (1848–1928).
4. Gomer.
5. Big Al.
6. Grizzly Hall is the home of eighteen bear performers.
7. Melvin the moose, Buff the buffalo, and Max the stag.
8. The island located in the middle of the Rivers of America has been at the Magic Kingdom since opening, but the attraction itself did not officially open until 1973.
9. Splash Mountain.
10. The small bear is known as Oscar.

Liberty Square

Questions

1. Which two presidents speak in the *Audio-Animatronics* attraction The Hall of Presidents?

2. What famous poet provides the narration for The Hall of Presidents?

3. What symbol located at The Hall of Presidents required an Act of Congress in order to be placed in the rotunda?

4. What is the name of the actor who serves as Your Ghost Host in the Haunted Mansion?

5. What is the name of the riverboat that sails the Rivers of America?

Liberty Square

Answers

1. Abraham Lincoln and Bill Clinton. The speaking role of President Lincoln was recorded by actor Royal Dano, who also provided the voice for the Disneyland attraction Great Moments with Mr. Lincoln. President Clinton himself was recorded for the attraction.

2. Maya Angelou provides the narration for The Hall of Presidents.

3. The Great Seal, which is located in the rotunda, required an Act of Congress for its approval. Only two other such seals exist, and they are located in the White House Oval Office in Washington, D.C., and at the Liberty Bell in Philadelphia, Pennsylvania.

4. Actor Paul Frees provides the narration in the Haunted Mansion. Many may recognize the voice of Frees from the animated cartoon series *The Bullwinkle Show*, in which he provided the voice of Boris Badenov.

5. The current name of the riverboat is the *Liberty Belle*. Previously it was known as the *Richard F. Irvine*.

Mickey's Toontown Fair

1. Mickey's Toontown Fair was formerly referred to by what other name?

2. Grandma Duck's Farm was replaced by which two attractions when Mickey's Toontown Fair opened?

3. Who moved in next door to Mickey when Mickey's Toontown Fair opened?

4. In what shape are the ride vehicles used in the miniature roller coaster attraction, The Barnstormer?

5. What is the name of the farm where The Barnstormer is located?

Mickey's Toontown Fair

Answers

1. Mickey's Toontown Fair officially opened in October 1996; the area was previously referred to as Mickey's Birthdayland and Mickey's Starland.
2. The petting farm known as Grandma Duck's Farm became the site for The Barnstormer and also Donald's Boat, the S.S. *Miss Daisy.*
3. Minnie Mouse now makes her home next to Mickey.
4. The ride vehicles are in the shape of biplanes.
5. Goofy's Wise Acres Farm is the site of the attraction, The Barnstormer.

Magic Kingdom Potpourri

Questions

1. How many total acres were originally purchased by Walt and Roy Disney when the park opened?

2. What is the official name of the nine-acre underground system of tunnels connecting all areas of the Magic Kingdom?

3. Which themed land exclusive to the Walt Disney World Magic Kingdom was originally planned for Disneyland in the 1950s?

4. What is "forced perspective"?

5. What does the acronym D.A.C.S. stand for and why is it important to the Magic Kingdom?

6. Why did Walt Disney World open in the month of October?

7. When the Magic Kingdom officially opened, how many attractions were available to those first visitors?

8. What was the price of a seven-ride coupon book when the Magic Kingdom first opened?

9. What famous Conductor led the World Symphony Orchestra during the Magic Kingdom's official dedication ceremonies?

10. Where is the official dedication plaque located in the Magic Kingdom?

Magic Kingdom Potpourri

Answers

1. Walt Disney had created several companies to help acquire the land he needed anonymously. In total there were 27,443 acres or 43 square miles of property purchased at a cost of a little more than $5 million. To put in perspective how much that equals, it is equivalent to the city of San Francisco or twice the size of Manhattan. Today, The Walt Disney Company owns over 30,000 acres.

2. The tunnel system is officially referred to as the Utilidors. In fact, it isn't really an underground tunnel. When the Magic Kingdom was built, it was quickly realized that the high water table in Florida would not support an underground system, so the Utilidors are actually on the ground level and the Magic Kingdom is situated on the second level. The idea behind the Utilidors came when Walt Disney observed one day the paradox of a cast member dressed as a Frontierland cowboy walking through Tomorrowland.

3. Liberty Square was originally planned for Disneyland.

4. Forced perspective is an architectural trick used by Disney designers in the Magic Kingdom to make the buildings appear taller than they actually are. Windows, balconies, and furniture were all shrunk on the second floors and even more on the third floors to create the illusion.

5. D.A.C.S. is short for Digital Animation Control System. D.A.C.S. is the computer center for the Magic Kingdom, the nerve center that virtually controls everything in the park from the hundreds of audio recordings to the opening and closing of attraction doors.

6. The month of October was chosen because that month had always statistically been Disneyland's least congested time of the year. With that in mind, Disney officials decided to open the park on October 1, 1971, so it could successfully deal with any problems that might arise during its first days.

7. When the Magic Kingdom opened, there were only twenty-two attractions available. The Magic Kingdom now features over forty attractions.

8. The price of a seven-ride coupon book was $4.75.

9. Even though the Magic Kingdom opened on October 1, 1971, the "official" dedication took place on October 25, 1971. Arthur Fiedler conducted the World Symphony Orchestra on its day of dedication.

10. The official dedication plaque is located next to the Town Square flagpole.

Epcot

Future World

Questions

1. How many legs support Spaceship Earth?

2. The outside of Spaceship Earth is constructed of what material?

3. How many individual panels were combined to construct Spaceship Earth?

4. Guests are transported through Spaceship Earth in vehicles known as what?

5. What is the name of the interactive center guests visit after exiting the Spaceship Earth attraction?

6. What is the name of the hands-on exposition and display area that introduces guests to the world's newest products and inventions?

7. What is the name of the largest merchandise shop in Future World?

8. What is the name of the show staring Ellen DeGeneres in Universe of Energy?

9. What is the name of the fictitious company that sponsors the probe ship in Body Wars?

10. What is the name of the captain of the probe ship in Body Wars?

11. What is the name of the little flight instructor whose assignment it is to operate the brain of a young boy in Cranium Command?

12. What is the name of the general to whom guests are introduced during the preshow in Cranium Command?

13. What was the first Future World pavilion to be added after the park's official grand opening?

14. In which two attractions can you hear the song "There's a Great Big Beautiful Tomorrow"?

15. What is the name of the attraction that features a fast-paced behind-the scenes tour of an automotive research and development facility?

16. In The Living Seas, what are the elevators called that deposit guests at the ocean research center Sea Base Alpha?

17. Who is considered the Commander of Sea Base Alpha at The Living Seas?

18. The first manatee ever to be born in captivity at The Living Seas was in 1991. What name was given to the baby manatee?

19. Which Future World pavilion was the first to change its corporate sponsor?

20. What is the name of the new *Audio-Animatronics* show that replaced the Kitchen Kabaret?

21. What is the title of the film shown in The Land, which stars the characters from the 1994 full-length animated feature *The Lion King*?

22. What is the name of the hands-on display area located on the second level at the Journey into Imagination?

23. What is the name of the 3D film featured in Journey into Imagination?

24. What is the theme song for the Journey into Imagination attraction?

25. Which actress plays research scientist, Dr. Lair, in Body Wars?

Future World

Answers

1. Spaceship Earth, the world's largest geodesic sphere, is supported by six legs. Each leg is eighteen feet long and supports a structure that weighs approximately sixteen million pounds.

2. The outside of Spaceship Earth is made from a special aluminum called alucobond.

3. There are exactly 11,324 panels that make up Spaceship Earth.

4. Guests embark on their journey through the history of communication in "time machine" vehicles.

5. Global Neighborhood.

6. Innoventions.

7. Located in Innoventions East is the merchandise shop known as the Centorium.

8. Ellen stars in the show "Ellen's Energy Adventure." In the film, Ellen finds herself on the television show *Jeopardy*, pitted against her archrival and ex–college roommate, Dr. Judy Peterson, portrayed by actress Jamie Lee Curtis. She then joins the pavilion's guests in learning more about energy.

9. The company's name is Miniaturized Exploration Technologies. Its acronym, MET, represents a salute to the sponsor of the attraction Wonders of Life, Metropolitan Life.

10. Captain Braddock, portrayed by actor Tim Matheson, serves as the leader of the probe ship in Body Wars.

11. Buzzy.

12. General Knowledge.

13. Horizons was the first pavilion to be added to Future World, opening one year to the day after the official Epcot grand opening on October 1, 1982.

14. The song is the original theme song for the Tomorrowland attraction, Walt Disney's Carousel of Progress. In addition, the song can also be heard in the Future World attraction, Horizons. The song was written by the team of Richard and Robert Sherman for the Carousel of Progress, which made its original debut at the New York World's Fair in 1964–65, where it was referred to as Progressland.

15. The attraction is known as Test Track and it debuted in the spring of 1997. The World of Motion attraction originally occupied this site.

16. The elevators are referred to as hydrolators.
17. Commander Fulton.
18. After the birth of the manatee, a contest was held for Florida schoolchildren to select a name. The name CHESTER was chosen, which stands for; Children Helping Endangered Species To Eventually Recover.
19. In 1993, The Land's corporate sponsor changed from Kraft to Nestlé.
20. The musical concert Food Rocks replaced Kitchen Kabaret in 1994. The host for Food Rocks is Food Wrapper, voiced by rap singer Tone Loc. The show depicts parodies of many of the music industry's biggest stars such as Cher, The Beach Boys, and Sting.
21. Stars of The Lion King (1994) appear in their own environmental film known as The Circle of Life.
22. The Image Works.
23. The 3D film is called Honey, I Shrunk the Audience. The two feature films, Honey, I Shrunk the Kids (1989) and Honey, I Blew Up the Kid (1992), provided the inspiration for the attraction. Some member of the cast from the two films as well as actor Eric Idle star in Honey, I Shrunk the Audience.
24. The song is titled "One Little Spark" and was written by the team of Richard and Robert Sherman.
25. Actress Elizabeth Shue plays research scientist, Dr. Lair, in Body Wars. She has also appeared in three Disney films, Adventures in Babysitting (1987), Cocktail (1988), and The Marrying Man (1991).

World Showcase

Questions

1. What are the names of the two Plaza merchandise shops that mark the entrance to World Showcase?

2. The Victorian-style gardens featured at Canada are patterned after what famous botanical garden?

3. Where in Epcot can guests find Tudor Lane and High Street?

4. What is the name of the restaurant located on the second level of France?

5. Which is the only World Showcase country to represent the continent of Africa?

6. What orchestra provided the musical score and soundtrack for The American Adventure when it opened in 1982?

7. What is the name of the a cappella singing group that entertains guests with classic American songs in the rotunda of The American Adventure?

8. What is the name of the outdoor theater located on the lagoon side of The American Adventure?

9. Name the four U.S. presidents depicted in *Audio-Animatronics* form in The American Adventure.

10. Which pavilion is the most recent addition to the World Showcase collection of countries?

11. What is the shape of the ride vehicles used in Maelstrom?

12. Where can guests find the Puffin's Roost?

13. The main building that houses Mexico in World Showcase was inspired by what type of ancient temple?

14. What type of church is found at the entrance of the Norway pavilion?

15. Which Christmas tradition, originally begun at Disneyland in 1958, is celebrated at Epcot?

World Showcase

Answers

1. The two shops are called Disney Traders and Port of Entry.
2. The Butchart Gardens, located in British Columbia.
3. Tudor Lane and High Street are two of the quaint little streets that can be found in the United Kingdom.
4. Bistro de Paris.
5. Morocco.
6. The Philadelphia Orchestra recorded the music for The American Adventure. Forty-two years earlier, the Philadelphia Orchestra, led by conductor Leopold Stokowski, provided the musical score for the full-length animated feature *Fantasia* (1940).
7. The Voices of Liberty.
8. America Gardens.
9. George Washington and Thomas Jefferson are represented prior to their being elected as president. Theodore Roosevelt and Franklin D. Roosevelt are shown during their presidential terms.
10. Norway was the most recent addition to World Showcase, opening in 1988. Prior to that Morocco had been the most recent, in 1984.
11. A version of a traditional Viking ship serves as the ride vehicles in Maelstrom.
12. It is one of the merchandise shops in Norway, specializing in toys, games, and the trademark of Norway—trolls!
13. The main building that houses Mexico in World Showcase was inspired by the ancient Aztec pyramids.
14. A stave church is found at the entrance of the Norway pavilion.
15. The holiday tradition is the Candlelight Procession. A celebrity narrator tells the story of Christmas accompanied by a full orchestra and choir. The centerpiece of the celebration is a human Christmas tree formed by a Disney cast member volunteer choir.

Disney-MGM Studios

Questions

1. Why is a water tower the symbol for the Disney-MGM Studios?

2. What is the Disney-coined word that describes the performers who walk up and down the various streets at the Disney-MGM Studios and entertain guests?

3. One of the buildings that make up the Keystone Clothiers is patterned after what famous Hollywood landmark?

4. An *Audio-Animatronics* display of which popular MGM film appears at the conclusion of The Great Movie Ride?

5. Name the CBS television show whose footage was licensed to The Walt Disney Company for use in a popular Disney-MGM Studios attraction at the end of Sunset Boulevard.

6. What is the name of the hotel that serves as the home for The Twilight Zone Tower of Terror?

7. According to the storyline, when did the final guests check into the hotel, before it was struck by lightning and abandoned?

8. From what room of the hotel do guests board freight elevators for their journey into the "5th Dimension" on The Twilight Zone Tower of Terror?

9. What is the tallest attraction at the Walt Disney World Resort?

10. What is the name of the 1,500-seat amphitheater reminiscent of the famed Hollywood Bowl, which features daily musical performances?

11. What is the name of the merchandise shop located on Sunset Boulevard that is decorated with vintage Disney character merchandise?

12. Where can a guest find The Catwalk Bar?

13. Former 1993 Miss America, Leanza Cornett, had one of her early starring roles in which Disney-MGM Studios attraction?

14. What is the name of the captain in the attraction Voyage of The Little Mermaid?

15. Name the attraction that features a giant-sized filmstrip with a series of Mickeys cascading down the reel outside of its building.

16. What is the name of the short film that stars Robin Williams and Walter Cronkite?

17. What is the name of the fictitious oil company featured on the tanker truck in Catastrophe Canyon?

18. Name the restaurant that was originally known as The Studio Pizzeria.

19. What interactive entertainment facility and eatery was inspired by a 1995 Disney feature?

20. What are the names of the vehicles that guests use for their voyage in Star Tours?

21. What character serves as the projectionist for the film in *Muppet*Vision 3D*?

22. Which two characters disguise themselves as Mickey Mouse in *Muppet*Vision 3D*?

23. The characters Simon Wier and Lester Lucky appear in a film for which Disney-MGM Studios attraction?

24. What is the name of the merchandise shop inspired by the television show, *Ellen*?

25. What popular illusionist has The Walt Disney Company teamed up with to bring guests at the Disney-MGM Studios a new themed restaurant?

Disney-MGM Studios

Answers

1. A water tower was visible on the grounds of almost every California movie studio, the Disney Studio in Burbank being no exception. The reason was for convenience and safety. In most cases, California movie studios were built out beyond any developed cities' borders. Fire protection was an issue, with stages being constructed of wood, so the water tower was a necessity in case disaster struck.

2. The street entertainers are referred to as Streetmosphere. This entertaining group of performers don costumes appropriate to various themes, such as a policeman, cabdriver, starlet, autograph seeker, and gossip columnist.

3. The Max Factor Building.

4. An *Audio-Animatronics* display of characters from the film *The Wizard of Oz* (1939) appears at the conclusion of The Great Movie Ride.

5. Footage from the CBS television series *The Twilight Zone* was licensed by The Walt Disney Company for use in The Twilight Zone Tower of Terror.

6. The Hollywood Tower Hotel.

7. The hotel was struck by lightning and closed on October 31, 1939, exactly ten years after its official opening.

8. Bellhops eventually escort guests to the Boiler Room so they can enter freight elevators for the journey and plunge of their life.

9. The Twilight Zone Tower of Terror stands 199 feet. If it were any higher it would be "tagged" by FAA regulators and require a red flashing light to warn low-flying aircraft.

10. Located on Sunset Boulevard, the amphitheater is known as Theater of the Stars.

11. Once Upon a Time.

12. The Catwalk Bar is located on the second level above The Hollywood Brown Derby and the Soundstage Restaurant.

13. The former Miss America played Ariel in the Voyage of The Little Mermaid.

14. Captain Horatio Witherspoon.

15. The Magic of Disney Animation features the giant filmstrip.

16. The name of the short film is *Back to Neverland* and it is featured in The

Magic of Disney Animation. The film demonstrates the steps in the making of an animated film.

17. The fictitious company is known as the Mohave Oil Company.
18. The Studio Pizzeria became Mama Melrose's Ristorante Italiano.
19. *Toy Story* (1995) inspired the interactive entertainment facility and eatery known as Disney's Toy Story Pizza Planet Arcade.
20. The space-age vehicles are known as Star Speeders.
21. The Swedish Chef operates the "Yell and How" projector for the film *Muppet*Vision 3D*.
22. Rizzo the Rat disguises himself as Mickey Mouse during the preshow and the three-dimensional figure Waldo C. Graphic changes his appearance to resemble Mickey at the conclusion of the film in *Muppet*Vision 3D*.
23. The two characters appear in The Monster Sound Show. Lester Lucky is a representative from the Lucky Life Insurance Company, attempting to sell a policy to the sinister Simon Wier.
24. The merchandise shop is Buy the Book, and it was inspired by the bookstore of the same name featured on the television series, Ellen.
25. The Walt Disney Company has teamed up with illusionist David Copperfield. The restaurant is known as Copperfield Magic Underground and it is scheduled to open in 1998. The restaurant reflects the history and the mystery of magic and illusion.

Disneyland Paris

Questions

1. On which day did Disneyland Paris officially change its name from Euro Disneyland?

2. Disneyland Paris has a fleet of four train engines that make up the Disneyland Paris Railroad. What are each of the train carriages pulled by the train engines named after?

3. Where can guests discover a showroom featuring actual antique cars and automobile memorabilia?

4. Where can guests find Lucy the glass elephant?

5. What are the names of the two arcades behind the shops along Main Street, USA?

6. What type of creature lives in the basement of Sleeping Beauty Castle, known as Le Château de la Belle au Bois Dormant?

7. Which structure provided some of the inspiration for Sleeping Beauty Castle?

8. What is the only Disney attraction to be based on an Academy Award–winning animated short?

9. Which two attractions were inspired by the 1951 full-length animated feature *Alice in Wonderland*?

10. In 1994, two attractions opened in Disneyland Paris, known as Le Petit Train du Cirque and Le Pays des Contes de Fées. Which two Disneyland attractions in California are they patterned after?

11. Which aerial attraction has never been included in Disneyland Paris, even though the attraction was included in each of the other three Magic Kingdoms?

12. In which Disneyland Paris merchandise shop can you find a beanstalk growing inside?

13. What is the name of the legendary Old West town featured in Frontierland?

14. What is the Disneyland Paris equivalent to the Mike Fink Keel Boats?

15. How many different types of watercraft sail on the Rivers of the Far West?

16. What is the name of the tropical island located in Adventureland, with secret caverns, tunnels, waterfalls, and a suspension bridge?

17. From which restaurant can guests view part of Pirates of the Caribbean?

18. Which Disney attraction included the first looping track?

19. A recent addition to Disneyland Paris is the popular attraction Space Mountain. During its development, what was Space Mountain originally going to be called?

20. Which popular Adventureland attraction is featured in each of the other three Magic Kingdoms but not Disneyland Paris?

Disneyland
Paris

Answers

1. On October 1, 1994, Euro Disneyland officially changed its name to Disneyland Paris.
2. Each of the train cars is named after a place important in American history and culture, such as Boston, Coney Island, and Yorktown.
3. Antique cars and automobile memorabilia are featured at Main Street Motors.
4. Lucy the glass elephant can be found in the Main Street, USA, shop known as the Boardwalk Candy Palace. Lucy is actually a representation of the structure near Atlantic City, New Jersey. Another model of Lucy can also be found in the main lobby of Disney's BoardWalk Resort at the Walt Disney World Resort.
5. The two are known as Discovery Arcade and Liberty Arcade. The two areas were designed exclusively for Disneyland Paris as a way of providing additional shelter during inclement weather and providing rear entry to the different merchandise shops and restaurants. Discovery Arcade is dedicated to the imaginative spirit of people who turned dreams into reality. Liberty Arcade pays tribute to the Statue of Liberty located in New York Harbor.
6. Deep in the underground passages of the castle rests a dragon in its lair. When the dragon awakens, smoke comes from his nostrils. The area is known as the La Tanière du Dragon.
7. Sleeping Beauty Castle gained its inspiration from Austratio in medieval manuscripts and from the dreamlike architecture of Mont-Saint-Michel. Mont-Saint-Michel is situated on the Normandy coast. The structure was first designed as a church when it was built in 708 but was converted into an abbey in the year 966.
8. The 1937 Academy Award–winning short *The Old Mill* provides the inspiration for the attraction Les Pirouettes du Vieux Moulin. The attraction is a one-of-a-kind Ferris wheel.
9. The two attractions are the Mad Hatter's Teacups and Alice's Curious Labyrinth. The latter is unique to Disneyland Paris, being a hedge maze designed with complicated walkways that have Disney characters along the way.
10. Casey Jr. Circus Train and Storybook Land Canal Boats.

11. The Skyway was never included in Disneyland Paris.
12. The Brave Little Tailor Shop.
13. Thunder Mesa.
14. The River Rogue Keelboats.
15. Two—keelboats and authentic paddle wheelers.
16. Adventure Isle.
17. The Blue Lagoon Restaurant.
18. The first looping track was included on Indiana Jones et le Temple du Peril. This roller coaster attraction cascades through an archaeological dig site past ancient ruins of a Lost City.
19. Discovery Mountain.
20. The Jungle Cruise is not a Disneyland Paris attraction. Many European theme parks had already copied the concept so it would have been too familiar for guests.

Disney Resorts/ Other Attractions

Questions

1. What are the names of the three resort towers that make up the Disneyland Hotel in California?

2. What is the name of the nighttime entertainment water and musical show featured at the Disneyland Hotel in California?

3. What is the name of the state-created government entity that oversees the governmental needs of the Walt Disney World Resort?

4. When the Walt Disney World Resort opened in 1971, how many choices did guests have for accommodations if they wanted to stay on the property?

5. What is unique about the construction method used for Disney's Contemporary Resort?

6. Where can one find the Great Ceremonial House?

7. The nighttime water and musical show known as the Electrical

Water Pageant that performs daily on Bay Lake and Seven Seas Lagoon provided the inspiration for which Disneyland attraction?

8. Which nighttime entertainment show has been in existence longer, the Hoop Dee Doo Musical Revue, or the Polynesian Luau?

9. Which Disney resort doubled its capacity after its first year of operation?

10. Which individual won the first Walt Disney World Golf Classic held in 1971?

11. Which area was originally called Blackbeard's Island?

12. Which water park located at the Walt Disney World Resort is modeled after the good old-fashion' swimming hole?

13. What was the original name of the Disney Village Marketplace?

14. What is Ear Force One?

15. At which resort can guests enjoy English-style "high tea"?

16. Which Walt Disney World resort contains the largest number of rooms?

17. What is the name of the 2,100-foot water inner tube ride located at Typhoon Lagoon?

18. Where at Pleasure Island can you enjoy the entertainment of some of the industry's up-and-coming new comics?

19. Illusionist Doug Henning was hired as a consultant to assist in the development of what Pleasure Island attraction?

20. Where can guests experience the largest sand-bottom pool in the world?

21. Which resort opened first, Disney's Port Orleans, or Disney's Dixie Landings?

22. What are the names of the two golf courses that make up the Bonnet Creek Golf Club?

23. In which Disney resort can one find a restaurant known as Cafe Fantasia?

24. What is the tallest resort at Disneyland Paris?

25. Which Disneyland Paris resort is constructed entirely from stone and wood?

26. Which Disneyland Paris resort was inspired by the design of Disney's Yacht Club, located at the Walt Disney World Resort?

27. What is the name of the entertainment facility located at Disneyland Paris that consists of nightclubs, themed restaurants, and shops?

28. Which restaurant at the Disneyland Paris Resort was named after an original Mouseketeer?

29. What is the name of the Disneyland Paris dinner show that stars stunt riders, buffaloes, cavalcades, and horses?

30. The Shades of Green resort at Walt Disney World Resort used to be called what?

31. Which Walt Disney World resort opened twenty-four years after the original drawings for the resort were created?

32. What is the name of the man-made geyser located at Disney's Wilderness Lodge Resort?

33. Which animated character is considered the unofficial mascot for Disney's Wilderness Lodge Resort?

34. Besides football, baseball, and basketball, what two other themed buildings are represented at Disney's All-Star Sports Resort?

35. What are the five musical themes that are represented in buildings at Disney's All-Star Music Resort?

36. Name the six performers that star in the Hoop Dee Doo Musical Revue.

37. What is the name of the nine-hole executive golf course located next to Disney's Polynesian Resort?

38. What popular eatery and entertainment facility opened its star-studded doors in December of 1994 at Pleasure Island?

39. Where can guests experience the thrills of Mt. Gushmore and Summit Plummet?

40. What is the name of Blizzard Beach's mascot?

41. The Papeete Bay Verandah located at Disney's Polynesian Resort was replaced in 1995 with which popular interactive restaurant?

42. What is the name of the popular restaurant located on the top floor of Disney's Contemporary Resort, and what restaurant did it replace?

43. What is the name of the wedding studio located near Disney's Wedding Pavilion at the Walt Disney World Resort?

44. Which popular Disney Village Marketplace restaurant closed in 1995, only to reopen several months later at Disney's Contemporary Resort?

45. Where was the first resort opened by The Walt Disney Company beyond the borders of a Disney theme park?

46. The Walt Disney Company purchased the Pan Pacific Hotel, located near Disneyland and the Disneyland Hotel. After the purchase, the hotel's name was changed to what?

47. Which Walt Disney World resort changed its name completely in January 1996?

48. What is the name of the Disney resort located in South Carolina?

49. What is the name of the two miniature golf courses that opened in 1996 at the Walt Disney World Resort?

50. Disney's Yacht Club Resort, Disney's Beach Club Resort, and Disney's BoardWalk Resort are situated around which body of water?

51. Who was responsible for the architectural design of the 1930s-style seaside resort known as Disney's BoardWalk Resort?

52. What is the name of Walt Disney World Resort's first "sports club"?

53. What is the name of the 200-foot water slide, reminiscent of an old-fashioned wooden roller coaster, at Disney's BoardWalk Resort?

54. What is the name of the Disney Village Marketplace dining facility that allows guests to eat while situated in a tropical forest with birds, animals, and special effects of rain, lightning, and thunder?

55. What is the name of the largest merchandise shop located at the Walt Disney World Resort?

56. What is the name of the planned dining location at the Walt Disney World Resort that will have an all-sports-themed decor, and whose owners include sports celebrities Joe Montana, Monica Seles, André Agassi, Wayne Gretzky, Ken Griffey, Jr., and Shaquille O'Neal?

57. The eight-theater cinema located at the Disneyland Paris Resort is named after which famous nineteenth-century French film pioneer?

58. What is the name of the restaurant owned by superstar Gloria Estefan, which is scheduled to open in 1997 in The Westside at Downtown Disney?

59. What is the name of the European-inspired circus offering nightly performances at Downtown Disney?

60. Which Disney resort gained its inspiration from a 16th-Century Spanish explorer?

Disney Resorts/
Other Attractions

Answers

1. The three resort towers are the Marina, the Sierra, and the Bonita.
2. Fantasy Waters.
3. In 1967 the Reedy Creek Improvement District was created by the Florida legislature to oversee the governmental needs of the Walt Disney World Resort.
4. When the Walt Disney World Resort opened on October 1, 1971, guests could choose one of three accommodations: The Contemporary Resort, Polynesian Village, and Fort Wilderness. Today guests can choose from seventeen Disney resorts.
5. The A-Frame resort was built similar to an egg crate. The individual rooms were completed, and in some cases completely furnished, several miles away, then transported and slid into the hotel's structure.
6. The Great Ceremonial House is the main building of Disney's Polynesian Resort.
7. The Electrical Water Pageant debuted in 1971 and inspired the creation of the Main Street Electrical Parade, which marked its debut on June 17, 1972.
8. The Polynesian Luau has been in existence since 1971. The Hoop-Dee-Doo Musical Revue debuted in 1974. Over the years the names of the two shows have gone through changes. The Polynesian Luau has been called the Polynesian Revue and Kaui-Pono Polynesian Revue. The Hoop-Dee-Doo Musical Revue has been called the Country Hoedown and the Pioneer Hall Revue.
9. Disney's Fort Wilderness Resort Campground opened in 1971 and doubled its size by the end of 1972.
10. The annual PGA event was first won by Jack Nicklaus in 1971. Nicklaus successfully captured the top spot the first three years of the tournament.
11. Discovery Island, the 11.5-acre accredited zoological park, was previously called Treasure Island when it opened in 1974. Blackbeard's Island was the original name before the name Treasure Island was chosen.
12. Located next to Disney's Fort Wilderness Resort Campground is River Country, which opened in 1976.

13. The Lake Buena Vista Village was the original name of the shopping and dining area when it opened in 1975. The name then changed to the Walt Disney World Village before becoming the Disney Village Marketplace. In 1997 the Disney Village Marketplace became part of a new area known as Downtown Disney. Downtown Disney consists of three distinct and unique areas—Pleasure Island, Disney Marketplace, and The Westside.

14. Ear Force One is the name of the hot air balloon shaped like Mickey Mouse.

15. Guests can enjoy high tea at The Garden View Lounge, located in Disney's Grand Floridian Beach Resort.

16. The 2,112-room Disney's Caribbean Beach Resort, which opened in 1988.

17. Castaway Creek. A similar water ride at Blizzard Beach is known as Cross Country Creek.

18. The Comedy Warehouse.

19. The Adventurer's Club, which is styled after a 1930s private club.

20. The sand-bottom pool Stormalong Bay is located at Disney's Yacht and Beach Club Resorts. The pool stretches over three acres and is the common pool shared by both resorts.

21. Disney's Port Orleans Resort opened May 17, 1991, and Disney's Dixie Landings Resort opened almost a year later on February 2, 1992.

22. The Osprey Ridge and Eagle Pines Golf courses designed by professional golfers Tom Fazio and Pete Dye.

23. Cafe Fantasia is in the Disneyland Hotel at the Disneyland Paris Resort. This beautifully styled restaurant features characters from *Fantasia* (1940) in the decor.

24. The tallest Disneyland Paris resort is the 1930s-style Hotel New York.

25. The Sequoia Lodge is constructed entirely from stone and wood and is patterned after the lodges found in American national parks. A similar design and inspiration were used two years later for the Wilderness Lodge at the Walt Disney World Resort.

26. The Newport Bay Club.

27. Disney Village, formerly known as Festival Disney.

28. The 1950s-style soda shop is known as Annette's Diner. The restaurant itself is located in the Disney Village district and is named, of course, after original Mouseketeer Annette Funicello.

29. The popular dinner show is called Buffalo Bill's Wild West Show and is reminiscent of shows performed by the popular entertainer for Paris audiences in the 1880s.

30. Shades of Green at Walt Disney World Resort was known as The Disney Inn from 1986 to 1994. Prior to that the hotel was called the Golf Resort when it opened in 1973. The present resort is owned by the United States military for use by its personnel.

31. Plans for Disney's Wilderness Lodge Resort were created twenty-four years before the resort opened. The resort was inspired by the national park lodges of the Northwest such as those found in Yosemite and Yellowstone.

32. Firerock Geyser.

33. Humphrey, a grizzly bear whose career began in the 1950 animated short *Hold That Pose*, acts as the resort's unofficial mascot.

34. The resort's other two themes are surfing and tennis. The five different themes are known as Touchdown, Home Run Hotel, Hoops Hotel, Surf's Up, and Center Court.

35. The five different themes are Calypso, Rock, Jazz, Country, and Broadway.

36. Johnny Ringo, Jim Handy, Six Bits Slocum, Flora Long, Claire Delune, and Dolly Drew.

37. The nine-hole executive course is called the Oak Trail Golf Course.

38. Planet Hollywood opened its doors in 1994 at Pleasure Island. The 95-foot-high spherical building features movie memorabilia surrounding a 400-seat dining facility. Some of its celebrity owners include Arnold Schwarzenegger, Demi Moore, Bruce Willis, and Sylvester Stallone.

39. Blizzard Beach. Mt. Gushmore offers a variety of water slides, including moguls, slalom courses, and toboggan and water-sled runs. Summit Plummet boasts the world's tallest and fastest free-fall water slide.

40. The blue-colored alligator is named Ice Gator.

41. The new restaurant's name is 'Ohana, which means "family."

42. The popular restaurant is called the California Grill, and it replaced the Top of the World.

43. The wedding studio is called Franck's, named after the character portrayed by actor Martin Short in the films *Father of the Bride* and *Father of the Bride II*. The first couple exchanged their vows at Disney's Wedding Pavilion in June 1995.

44. Chef Mickey's.

45. Disney's Vero Beach Resort in Vero Beach, Florida, which opened October 1, 1995.

46. The Disneyland Pacific Hotel.

47. The Disney Vacation Club, which opened in 1991, changed its name to

Disney's Old Key West Resort in January, 1996. The resort represents Disney's first entry into vacation ownership and membership.

48. On March 1, 1996, Disney's Hilton Head Island Resort opened. The resort itself is composed of two different areas on Hilton Head Island: a beach house located right on the island's pristine beaches, and the resort accommodations, in an area known as Shelter Cove.

49. The two courses are known as Disney's Fantasia Gardens. The first course is traditional miniature golf, themed to the 1940 full-length animated feature *Fantasia*. The other is a miniature version of a real golf course. Both courses were designed by world-class architect Michael Graves. Graves's credits also include Hotel New York for Disneyland Paris, and the Swan and Dolphin Resorts at the Walt Disney World Resort.

50. Crescent Lake.

51. Architect and board member of The Walt Disney Company, Robert A. M. Stern. Stern is also credited with designing Disney's Yacht and Beach Club Resorts for the Walt Disney World Resort as well as the Newport Bay Club and Hotel Cheyenne for Disneyland Paris.

52. Located at Disney's BoardWalk Resort is the ESPN Club. Guests can catch all the action of their favorite teams and even meet some sports celebrities while at the ESPN Club.

53. The Keister Coaster.

54. The Rainforest Cafe.

55. The merchandise shop is known as the World of Disney and is located at the Disney Village Marketplace. The shop is nearly a football field in length and is composed of ten different themed rooms featuring character merchandise piled high to the ceiling.

56. The All-Star Cafe.

57. The French film producer and inventor Léon Gaumont lends his name to the eight-theater cinema known as Gaumont Cinema.

58. Bongos Cuban Cafe. In addition, famous restaurant owner and chef Wolfgang Puck and the House of Blues will have themed restaurants in The Westside.

59. The internationally recognized energy-packed show is known as Cirque du Soleil. The circus show's creator is Guy Laliberte.

60. Disney's Coronado Springs Resort, set to open in 1997, was inspired by the Spanish explorer, Francisco Vasquez de Coronado (1510–1554).

Walt Disney and His Legacy

Questions

1. What is the etymological derivation of the name Disney?

2. According to the story, after which friend of Elias and Flora Disney was Walt named?

3. Which of Walt's brothers was the only one not to have a birthday in the month of December?

4. Among the many business enterprises started by Walt's father, Elias, one was that of building contractor. Which individual helped Elias design and sketch plans for the homes he built?

5. Which fraternal organization did Walt Disney belong to when he was a teenager?

6. In which state, other than California, did Walt Disney live almost one fourth of his life?

7. What is the name of the theater to which Walt Disney sold animated cartoons while working for the Kansas City Film Ad Company?

8. What personal item did Walt sell in order to purchase a one-way railroad ticket from Kansas City to California so he could begin his new career?

9. In which branch of the military did Roy Disney serve?

10. How old was Walt Disney when Mickey Mouse made his theatrical debut?

11. Which Disney family member proposed to his girlfriend in a telegram?

12. After Walt Disney lost his rights to the animated character Oswald, what legendary entertainer advised Walt that if he wanted to protect his company and interests, he would have to "own every picture" he made?

13. What historical event did Walt Disney often refer to as his greatest ally in developing and establishing his talented staff of animators and artists during the 1930s?

14. With whom did Walt Disney sign his first major merchandising contract in an effort to market Disney characters?

15. What company during the 1930s was licensed to manufacture Mickey Mouse radios in the United States?

16. What company produced the first Disney phonograph record?

17. Walt Disney signed an exclusive two-year agreement with what company, giving him sole cartoon rights to a revolutionary new technology in the development of color?

18. Besides the site of the 1930s film studio, name some other Disney uses of the word *Hyperion*?

Walt Disney and His Legacy

19. Which character did not appear on a wristwatch during the 1930s: Mickey Mouse, Minnie Mouse, Donald Duck, or the Big Bad Wolf?

20. During his lifetime, Walt Disney crushed four cervical vertebrae as a result of an injury from what sport?

21. Who were Arrow, June, Nana, Pardner, Slim, Tacky, and Tommy?

22. Which aircraft company occupied space on the Disney Studio lot during World War II?

23. What entertainment mogul and millionaire offered to sell his ownership of RKO Pictures to Roy for the sum of one dollar?

24. Who were the original members of the Walt Disney Studio–created musical group, the Firehouse Five Plus Two?

25. What was the name of the organization formed by Disney employees that was meant to provide financial support for the construction of Disneyland?

26. What was Walt Disney referring to by "Daddy's day?"

27. What was considered Walt Disney's favorite themed land at Disneyland?

28. To which royal couple did Walt Disney present a gold-framed animation cel from the full-length film *Lady and the Tramp* (1955) on the occasion of their marriage?

29. What was the name of the ranch in Palm Springs where Walt and his family owned a vacation home?

30. Walt Disney served as grand marshal for what famous rodeo?

31. According to the composers, which song from the feature film *Mary Poppins* (1964) was considered Walt Disney's favorite song?

32. What did Walt Disney insist that each and every employee call him?

33. What was the name of the Denver, Colorado, sports facility owned by a group of celebrity investors including Walt Disney?

34. What popular science fiction writer once encouraged Walt Disney to run for mayor of Los Angeles?

35. In 1965, Walt Disney purchased property in California with the hopes of developing it into an alpine resort complete with hotels, restaurants, and a skating rink. What is the name of the area of Walt Disney's purchase?

36. What gave Walt Disney his inspiration for the *Audio-Animatronics* figures?

37. In 1965, Walt Disney formed a subsidiary named MAPO to handle new technologies such as *Audio-Animatronics*. What does MAPO stand for?

38. Walt Disney was presented with more Academy Awards than any other individual. Did Walt Disney ever present an Academy Award during his lifetime?

39. According to many accounts, what was Walt Disney's favorite food?

40. Name the schools of higher education that bestowed on Walt Disney honorary degrees during his lifetime.

41. What European city changed the name of one of its streets from Dunghill Lane to Disney Street?

42. Which two countries honored Walt Disney with the Order of the Cross and the Order of the Aztec Eagle?

43. How many feature films were released by Walt Disney Studios during Walt Disney's lifetime?

44. What famous child star later served on the Board of Directors for The Walt Disney Company?

45. What is the name of the Northern California winery that members of the Disney family purchased in 1976?

46. Which two Disney theme parks opened in the month of April?

47. Michael Eisner, prior to becoming the chief executive officer and chairman of the board of The Walt Disney Company, came from what other motion picture studio?

48. Since its formation as a company on October 16, 1923, by how many different names has The Walt Disney Company been known over the years?

49. What animated character holds the office of "treasurer" for the Disney Mint, a title featured on each Disney Dollar?

50. What is the name of the Disney record division formed in 1990 featuring contemporary music?

51. In what month and year did *Disney Adventures* magazine make its debut?

52. What word is used to describe the collecting of Disney memorabilia?

53. What is the name of the Disney business division created in 1994 responsible for the development of computer software products?

54. In what year did the town of Celebration, Florida, officially establish itself as a community?

55. What distinctive item of headgear is the focal point of the Feature Animation Building, which opened at the Disney Studios in Burbank in 1994?

56. In 1993, The Walt Disney Company purchased the rights to what New York–based film company?

57. The Walt Disney Gallery opened its first store in which city?

58. In 1994, Walt Disney Records released its first Latin music compilation, featuring the talents of Plácido Domingo and José Feliciano, among others. What is its title?

59. In 1995, The Walt Disney Company purchased what television network and its subsidiaries?

60. What is the name given to The Disney Store that represents the company's first venture into New York City?

61. What are the names of the two ocean liners that compose the Disney Cruise Line fleet?

62. What is the name of the 1,000-acre private Bahamian island purchased by The Walt Disney Company to support the Disney Cruise Line?

63. What is the name of the new theme park scheduled to open next to Disneyland?

64. The largest Disney theme park in the world will open in the spring of 1998 at Walt Disney World Resort. What is its name?

65. What is the name of the new Disney theme park scheduled to open next to Tokyo Disneyland?

Walt Disney
and His Legacy

Answers

1. The name Disney is derived from the word d'Isigny, referring to someone from the French Normandy coastal town, Isigny-sur-mer.
2. Reverend Walter Parr.
3. Roy was the only one of the Disney sons not to have a birthday in December; his birthday was in June. Walt, Herbert, and Raymond were all born in December.
4. Walt's mother, Flora.
5. DeMolay.
6. Missouri.
7. Newman Theater.
8. Walt sold his camera so he could raise enough money to take him to California.
9. Roy Disney served in the United States Navy during World War I.
10. Walt was only twenty-six!
11. Roy Disney used a telegram when he asked Edna Francis to marry him.
12. Charlie Chaplin.
13. The Great Depression gave Walt Disney the opportunity to capture the brightest and best talents in the field of animation because the poor economy made jobs scarce.
14. In 1930, Walt Disney signed his first major merchandising contract with George Borgfeldt of New York to manufacture and sell figurines and toys that bore the likeness of Mickey and Minnie. Two years later Walt signed a new and even more extensive contract with Herman "Kay" Kamen.
15. Emerson.
16. RCA Victor.
17. Technicolor.
18. The Hyperion Cafe is located in Disneyland Paris; the airship in the feature film *Island at the Top of the World* (1974); the publishers of this book, a division of The Walt Disney Company; and the name of a bungalow at the Disney Studios in Burbank used for meetings.
19. Minnie Mouse.
20. Polo.
21. The seven represented Walt Disney's stable of polo ponies.

22. Lockheed.

23. Howard Hughes.

24. The group was led by Ward Kimball and included Ed Penner, Harper Goff, Jimmy Macdonald, Frank Thomas, Clarke Mallery, and Danny Alguire. Between 1949 and 1970, the group produced twelve albums.

25. The name of the organization was the Disneyland Backers and the Boosters, formed by Disney Studio employee Hazel George. George organized the group after it became apparent that Walt and Roy Disney were running into opposition while trying to raise enough capital for the new theme park from traditional banking sources. Walt was encouraged by their support.

26. "Daddy's day" was always Sunday for Walt Disney. It represented the day when he would take his two children to area amusement parks, zoos, and carnivals. Walt Disney credits that experience with helping him develop his basis for the Disneyland theme park. Walt questioned why there couldn't be a place where children and adults could go together and all enjoy their day.

27. According to many reports, Walt Disney's favorite themed land was Fantasyland.

28. Princess Grace and Prince Rainier of Monaco.

29. The Smoke Tree Ranch.

30. The Calgary Stampede.

31. The song "Feed the Birds" has often been considered Walt Disney's favorite. The song was written by the team of Richard and Robert Sherman.

32. Walt Disney insisted that each and every employee call him by his first name, Walt.

33. The Celebrity Sports Center. The Walt Disney Company later bought the center and used it as a training ground for cast members soon to be operating resorts at Walt Disney World. The company sold the center in 1979.

34. Ray Bradbury.

35. Mineral King valley.

36. One day Walt Disney discovered a miniature animated mechanical bird over one hundred years old in an New Orleans antique shop. Walt purchased the mechanical bird and showed it to Roger Broggie, head of the machine shop. Walt asked Broggie to use updated technologies to develop life-sized birds that would be capable of moving and talking.

37. MAPO was developed as a subsidiary of WED Enterprises, known today as Walt Disney Imagineering. MAPO is an abbreviation for Mary

Poppins, a name coined after the success of that film. The subsidiary was created in part to handle the new technology developed in the 1960s called *Audio-Animatronics*.

38. Yes. Walt Disney presented Academy Awards in three different years—1936, 1942, and 1952. In 1936 Walt Disney performed the rare feat of actually making the presentation of the Academy Award for Best Short Cartoon to himself, for the animated short *The Country Cousin*.

39. Walt Disney's favorite food was a serving of chili and beans. In addition, Walt also enjoyed a piece of banana cream pie.

40. Walt Disney received honorary degrees from Harvard, Yale, UCLA, and USC.

41. London.

42. Walt Disney received Thailand's Order of the Cross and Mexico's Order of the Aztec Eagle.

43. Eighty-one.

44. Shirley Temple (Black) served briefly on the Board of Directors for Walt Disney Productions in 1974 and 1975. Walt Disney Productions changed its name to The Walt Disney Company in 1986.

45. In 1976, the Disney family purchased the Silverado Winery, located in the fabled Stag's Leap district of northern California.

46. Tokyo Disneyland and Disneyland Paris both opened in April.

47. Paramount.

48. Including its current name, a total of four. Beginning in 1923, the company was called the Disney Brothers Cartoon Studio. In 1926, the name changed to the Walt Disney Studio. In 1929, the company's name again changed to Walt Disney Productions. The next change did not occur until 1986, when it became The Walt Disney Company.

49. Scrooge McDuck.

50. Hollywood Records.

51. The first issue of the children's monthly magazine *Disney Adventures* was published in November 1990.

52. The word *Disneyana* is used to describe the collecting of Disney keepsakes.

53. Disney Interactive.

54. In 1994, the town of Celebration officially established itself as a community. The first residents moved in two years later.

55. The Sorcerer's hat from the full-length animated feature *Fantasia* (1940).

56. Miramax.

57. The first store opened in 1994 at the MainPlace Mall in Santa Ana,

California. The Gallery specializes in Disney art and collectibles based on Disney feature films and characters.

58. *Navidad en las Americas.*

59. The Walt Disney Company announced the purchase of Capital Cities/ABC, owner of the ABC-TV network on July 31, 1995. Coincidentally, as a result of the purchase, The Walt Disney Company also acquired the *Kansas City Star*, a newspaper Walt used to deliver when he was a nine-year-old boy.

60. The store is known as the House of Disney. It's storyline reveals that the 711 Fifth Avenue location represents the mansion of both Walt and Roy Disney. As the tale goes, Walt and Roy used the mansion whenever they visited New York to enjoy the latest Mickey Mouse cartoon at its celebrated gala premiere.

61. *Disney Magic* and *Disney Wonder* are the two ocean liners that make up the Disney Cruise Line. Each ship weighs in excess of 85,000 tons and was built at the Fincantieri Shipyards in Trieste, Italy. The ship's colors are black, white, yellow, and red, the same as Mickey Mouse.

62. Disney's Castaway Cay. Before Disney changed the name, it had been known as Gorda Cay.

63. Disney's California Adventure is the new park scheduled to open shortly after the turn of the century. The park will be themed to celebrate the fun and variety of California, its people, its accomplishments, and its unique places, from the glamour of Hollywood to the majesty of Yosemite National Park.

64. Disney's Animal Kingdom. When complete, the theme park will be five times larger than the Magic Kingdom. The park will combine thrilling attractions and exotic landscapes.

65. Tokyo DisneySea will open sometime during 2000.